Man against Mass Society

Other Titles of Interest from St. Augustine's Press and Dumb Ox Books

Gabriel Marcel, *The Mystery of Being* (in two volumes)
Jacques Maritain, *Natural Law*
Yves R. Simon, *The Great Dialogues of Nature and Space*
Richard Peddicord, O.P., *The Sacred Monster of Thomism: An Introduction to the Life and Legacy of Reginald Garrigou-Lagrange,* O.P.
John Paul II, *The John Paul II LifeGuide*™
Josef Pieper and Heinz Raskop, *What Catholics Believe*
Josef Pieper, *Scholasticism: Personalities and Problems*
Josef Pieper, *The Silence of St. Thomas*
Josef Pieper, *The Concept of Sin*
Josef Pieper, *Death and Immortality*
C.S. Lewis, *The Latin Letters of C.S. Lewis*
James V. Schall, S.J., *The Sum Total of Human Happiness*
James V. Schall, S.J., *The Regensburg Lecture*
Peter Kreeft, *The Philosophy of Jesus*
Peter Kreeft, *Jesus-Shock*
Servais Pinckaers, O.P., *Morality: The Catholic View*
Dietrich von Hildebrand, *The Heart: An Analysis of Human and Divine Affectivity*
Dietrich von Hildebrand, *The Dietrich von Hildebrand LifeGuide*™
Florent Gaboriau, *The Conversion of Edith Stein*
Ralph McInerny, *The Defamation of Pius XII*
Aristotle, *Aristotle – On Poetics*
Plato, *The Symposium of Plato: The Shelley Translation*
St. Augustine, *On Order [De Ordine]*
St. Augustine, *The St. Augustine LifeGuide*™
Thomas Aquinas, *Commentary on the Epistle to the Hebrews*
Thomas Aquinas, *Commentaries on St. Paul's Epistles to Timothy, Titus, and Philemon*
Thomas Aquinas, *Commentary on Aristotle's Nicomachean Ethics*
Thomas Aquinas, *Commentary on Aristotle's De Anima*
Thomas Aquinas, *Commentary on Aristotle's Metaphysics*
Thomas Aquinas, *Commentary on Aristotle's Posterior Analytics*
Thomas Aquinas, *Commentary on Aristotle's Physics*
Thomas Aquinas, *Disputed Questions on Virtue*
John of St. Thomas, *Introduction to the Summa Theologiae of Thomas Aquinas*
John Poinsot, *Tractatus de Signis*
Francisco Suarez, *On Creation, Conservation, & Concurrence*
Francisco Suarez, *Metaphysical Demonstration of the Existence of God*
Henry of Ghent, *Henry of Ghent's Summa of Ordinary Questions: Article One: On the Possibility of Human Knowledge*

Man against Mass Society

Gabriel Marcel

Translated by G. S. Fraser

Foreword by Donald MacKinnon

ST. AUGUSTINE'S PRESS
South Bend, Indiana

Originally published in America by the Henry Regnery Company in 1952.

Manufactured in the United States of America.

2 3 4 5 20 19 18 17 16 15

Library of Congress Cataloging in Publication Data
Marcel, Gabriel, 1889-1973.
[Hommes contre l'humain. English]
Man against mass society / Gabriel Marcel; foreword by Donald MacKinnon.
p. cm.
Reprint. Originally published: South Bend, Ind.: Gateway Editions, 1978.
ISBN-13: 978-1-58731-490-2 (pbk.: alk. paper)
ISBN-10: 1-58731-490-8 (pbk.: alk. paper)
1. Human beings. 2. Mass society. I. Title.
B2430.M253H5813 2008
128 - dc22 2008005832

∞ The paper used in this publication meets the minimum requirements of the American National Standard for Information Sciences – Permanence of Paper for Printed Materials, ANSI Z39.48-1984.

St. Augustine's Press
www.staugustine.net

CONTENTS

FOREWORD

THIS BOOK emphatically demands cooperation from its readers. M. Marcel sets his face steadfastly against any kind of abstract or generalized exposition: he invites his readers to enter into his conversation with himself, and if they are not prepared to bear the strain of its development, they had best not read him at all.

Further, although Marcel does not flaunt himself before his readers, he is not afraid to draw on his own experience in the last twenty years to give strength of outline to his argument. He does not claim for that experience a universal validity: he explicitly repudiates the title of inspired prophet. But he argues that these things of which he speaks are discernible in the society of his day, and more important, in his own heart. He admits that the title 'néo-Socratisme' agrees with his proposed philosophic aim: and therefore it is fair, I think, to ask of his book whether or no it deepens our self-knowledge. The critic may well quarrel with his indictment of the French *petits fonctionnaires*; but such quarrels are not fundamental. The question the reader must ask is the extent to which this book has shown him more clearly to himself.

And here it seems to me that if that reader is honest, he must admit that the author has indeed cast light in dark places. If M. Marcel's intellectual comprehension of Marxism lags behind that of, *e.g.*, R. P. Desroches or M. Merleau Ponty, he sees the essentially monstrous character of the claim to find in something called the 'march of history' the justification of every sort of cruelty. With a beautiful precision he reveals how the Left no less than the Right can count in its ranks men ready to apologize for, if not to justify, every form of brutality and foulness which 'progress' (the Left's counterpart of 'tradition') can somehow justify. There is a deep, albeit unrecognized kinship between the man who in 1937 was denying, or justifying, the massacre of Guernica, and the man who in 1947 is justifying, or denying Stalinist deportations and slave camps;

('progress' and 'tradition' are excellent examples of the sort of abstraction from whose tyranny M. Marcel would free us).

A man who writes as M. Marcel does is vulnerable in many places: he is admittedly diffuse in style, and he would admit the reality of his own personal prejudices. But as we follow the arguments of his book, our many differences with him are subdued by his own demanding honesty of mind. One is impelled to a self-scrutiny as rigorous as his own: where has one oneself compromised reverence for the mystery of human existence by acceptance of that which is shallow and superficial, tawdry and unclean? His book demands to be read as a summons to *exetasis biou*. He writes of fanaticism and violence, of lawlessness and partisanship not as forces externally arrayed against us, still less as abstract intellectual attitudes, but as dispositions of our own heart and will, formed unnoticed but suddenly revealed within us.

He may exaggerate: but the plight of a deeply religious humanism such as he delineates is nearly on all fours with that of the liberalism so painfully defended by Mr Irwin Shaw's hero in his remarkable novel *The Troubled Air*, Cape, 1951. I say nearly: for in the end, Marcel's deep faith suffuses his sombre judgment with a vista of continuing hope. He writes with a delicate profundity of such fundamental theological themes as grace and the *parousia*. To the man of faith comes repeatedly the assurance that the horizons of our age of violence are not the boundaries of the world as it is. (It would be fascinating to develop the similarity and contrast, between Marcel's teaching here and that of Albert Camus in his *L'Homme Révolté*, Gallimard, 1951.

Such work as M. Marcel's is very different from philosophy as received to-day in academic circles in this country. But like men of a very different school, he is at war with illusion and confusion; the often unsuspected contradictions in our assumptions about the world, the precariousness of our purchase-hold on our humanity, these are the things he wants us to see, and no longer escape the enquiry by sonorous and empty verbiage. We must come to ourselves, where we are: that coming is action, and in places he reminds us that it may be passion too. For 'what shall it profit a man if he gain the whole world and lose his own soul?' There will be those undoubtedly for whom, in no spirit of Stoic detachment and self-possession the imperative is clear to count the world nothing compared to that final eschatological integrity, in respect of such a concrete issue as the methods of modern warfare; the atomic, hydrogen and napalm bomb, to say nothing of the bacteriological warfare to which M. Marcel refers. If his sentiments are not infrequently conservative, the movement of this thought is rather in the direction of a spiritual radicalism more inflexible and more searing than the merely political in as much as it touches the very springs of intellect, imagination and will; its theological counterpart might well be that 'eschatological humanism' of which men like R. P. Louis Bouyer have written, *cf.* his *Le Sens de la Vie Monastique*, Editions Brepols, Turnhout et Paris, 1951.

1952. D. M. MACKINNON

PREFACE

THE UNIVERSAL AGAINST THE MASSES

BEFORE I do anything else, I should like to correct a misunderstanding. There is a mistake I have repeatedly observed men making who are genuinely in touch with my purely philosophical work and who have even acknowledged that they find in that work food for thought. In many cases, such readers have fancied that my attitudes towards the facts of social and political life have no real connection with that body of philosophical thought which I should rather, on the whole, *not* call my 'doctrine'. Such readers have thought it possible to make a sharp, almost surgical division between what, quite wrongly, they have considered as two quite separate parts of my work. I should like to say here as flatly as possible that such a severance is not, from my own point of view, permissible, and that between the two sections of my work which men seek to dissociate in this arbitrary fashion there exists, on the contrary, an unbreakable link. One might sum up this matter, or so it seems to me, in the following way.

The dynamic element in my philosophy, taken as a whole, can be seen as an obstinate and untiring battle against the spirit of abstraction. Since the years 1911 and 1912, the time of my first researches and my still unpublished earliest philosophical writings, I have played the part of a prosecuting counsel against every philosophy that seemed to me to remain the prisoner of abstractions. Was this attitude, in these early days, a result of Bergson's influence? I should not like to swear to it, one way or the other, but it may well have been so. But this distrust of abstractions explains, for instance, the fascination which the Hegelian system exercised on me for such a long time. For, in spite of appearances to the contrary, Hegel did make a very splendid effort to preserve the primacy of the concrete; and no philosopher has protested more strongly against the confusion of the concrete with the immediately given. My severe and hostile criticism, on the other hand, of a pseudo-philosophy like that of Julien Benda is to be explained by the fundamentally abstract trend of Benda's thinking; he has never even suspected the existence of the true philosopher's urgent inner need to grasp reality in its concreteness.

On the other hand, this hostility of mine towards the spirit of abstraction is quite certainly *also* at the roots of the feeling of distrust aroused in me, not exactly by democracy itself, but by the sort of ideology which claims to justify democracy on philosophical grounds. At no time in my life, for instance, has the French Revolution inspired in me anything at all akin to admiration or even attachment; one reason may be that, when I was still very young, I became aware of the ravages in French social life that are due to a sort of egalitarian bigotry. But another feeling had its effect. It was also when I was still very young that my parents—for what reason, I am still not too clear—compelled me to read Mignet's very dry history of that great event; and the other feeling, which that reading aroused, was my innate horror of violence, disorder, cruelty. At that time, the glaring abuses in French social and political life which had dragged on *until* 1789 struck less feelingly home to me than the crimes of the Terror. Naturally, as time went on, I arrived at a more just or at least more balanced estimate of the French Revolution. But the feelings of indignation which the September Massacres and the other mass crimes of the Revolutionary period aroused in me in adolescence, were not, in the end, *essentially* very different from those much more recently aroused by the horrors of Stalinism or Nazism, or even by the shameful aspects of a purge nearer home.

Can there be any doubt, then, that a bent of mind so deeply rooted is the point of departure of my whole philosophical development? But my readers, very naturally, will want to ask me if there is any connection *that can be grasped* between my horror of abstraction and my horror of mass violence. My answer is that such a connection does certainly exist. Even for myself, however, it existed for a long time below the level of conscious understanding. It is, certainly, only at a fairly recent date that it has become explicit for me:

since, as I hope to show in detail in the present volume, the spirit of abstraction is essentially of the order of the passions, and since conversely, on the other hand, it is passion, not intelligence, which forges the most dangerous abstractions. Now, I can say without hesitation that my own thought has always been directed by a passionate love (but passionate at another level) for music, harmony, peace. And when I was still very young I grasped the truth that it is impossible to build true peace on abstractions; though I grasped it, of course, in a form that had not yet reached the stage of conceptual elaboration. (In passing, the fact that it is impossible to build true peace on abstractions is the deepest reason for the failure of the League of Nations, and of other pretentious organizations which resemble it). Perhaps also the sort of prejudice which I have always had in favour of Christianity, even during the very long period in which I could not envisage the possibility of becoming a practising and confessing Christian, may be explained by the unconquerable conviction I had that, so long as Christianity remained true to itself, Christianity could be the only authentic peacemaker.

A reader may ask, 'But so far as that goes, Christians of the Left think as you do; and is it not perfectly permissible to suppose that a Christianity of the Right will always remain conformist in spirit, that its essence is to try to appease and to manage by tact those who hold power in the world, or even to lean on them for support?' To that my answer would be that in fact I have always been extremely suspicious of a Christianity of the Right—I have always thought that such a Christianity runs the risk of distorting in the most sinister fashion the true message of Christ. (I have even been tempted to adopt as my own certain phrases of Pascal Laumière's, from the final act of my play, *Rome n'est plus dans Rome*). Only, I should like to add immediately that the men of the Right are very far from having a monopoly of the spirit of conformity and appeasement: there is a conformism of the Left, there are men of the Left who hold power in the world, there are 'right-thinking people' (in the conformist sense of the phrase) on the Left as well as the Right; I remember one day before the war saying something of this sort at the Ambassadeurs, thus greatly shocking Jacques and Raïssa Maritain.

One must add that conformism of the Left, not only because it has, if I may put it so, the wind behind its sails these days, but because it is in such glaring contradiction with the principles that the Left claims to be defending, must be denounced just as ruthlessly as conformism of the Right. Not, of course—this hardly needs saying—that there is any excuse for allowing conformism of the Right, with all it too often implies of blindness and unconscious cruelty, to cash in on that weight of reprobation with which, on this count, one must load the shoulders of the Left. One must recognize the fact that, in certain countries of Europe and the Americas, the spirit of clericalism, with the hateful political connivances that it implies, is tending to take on a character that, for a truly Christian conscience, becomes more and more offensive. The note of a truly honest mode of thinking in these matters, as in book-keeping, is to have a system of double entry, and to prohibit oneself from marking down—by an intellectually fraudulent operation—to the credit of the Right what one has to mark down to the debit of the Left. I am thinking now of people who, because of their horror of the Soviet world, are to-day tending to regard Nazism with a certain retrospective tolerance. That is an aberration—and a criminal aberration. In any case, who could fail to see at once the simple mechanism of the mental conjuring trick by which we belittle a danger that is past, simply because it *is* past, or because we believe it past? Is it really past? Or may it not in fact appear again, and in a form not radically altered? In this realm of discourse, we must learn once more to express ourselves categorically and to denounce the errors of a moral relativism which is, as may be easily shown, radically self-centred. Human nature being what it is, the movement which I condemn morally is too often the movement which hurts me personally; and I am likely to go on condemning it for so long as (and just for so long as) it is really able to hurt me.

But having said this, I should add immediately that there is an historical dogmatism no less disastrous in its consequences than this self-centred moral relativism. Simone de Beauvoir wrote a few years ago that crimes against the common law—crimes, that is, against person and property—ought not to be judged with too much severity; but that political crimes, on the other hand, are inexpiable. Such an assertion, as soon as one reflects on it a little, opens out gulfs beneath one's feet; it can be properly understood only if one lays bare the dogmatic philosophy of history which it presupposes. If political crime is a mortal sin, the reason must be that it goes against the meaning of history and that the latter, of course, is supposed to be generally known. To the already rather odd maxim, ' Nobody is assumed to be ignorant of the law', we must now add another even odder: 'Nobody is assumed to be ignorant of the meaning of history'. From the point of view of somebody like Simone de Beauvoir, an ordinary crime against person or property has no interest for history, it exists on the margin of history, and counts, so to say, as a merely venial sin. To be sure, we are all perfectly well aware that to a certain type of philosophic man of letters to-day those whom we call criminals often appear as extremely attractive: the novels and characters of Jean Genêt are a striking case in point. From such a novelist's point of view, a middle-class hero practising the dreary virtues of his retrograde social group is a much less brilliant character than a thief and pervert who has the courage to put into action those desires which, for the plodding *bourgeois*, never get beyond the stage of unadmitted day-dreams. I am thinking for instance of a play I propose to write in which we see a young married woman, all keyed up, confronting her husband, who is just about to play the host, with all the respect due to such a personage, to a rival and imitator of M. Jean Genêt, with this question: 'Tell me, Jo: can you swear to me that in the presence of Jacques Framboise, who has just come out of prison, you experience nothing that at all resembles a feeling of superiority?' Jo, confused and quite taken aback, remains silent. The lady presses her point: 'Answer me, Jo: the whole future of our relations depends on your answer'. In her discreet way, she then adds that Jo ought to feel a little ashamed, if anything, of wearing the white flower of a, legally at least, blameless life . . . If I have allowed myself a somewhat farcical digression here, it is to throw a clearer light on those generally inverted values which a contemporary literary *élite*—an international *élite*, too—is rapidly to-day tending to adopt for its own. And here, also, we find conformism and ' right-thinking persons'. One would be judged a 'wrong-thinking person' in such circles if one persisted in pointing out that theft, in itself, is a reprehensible act. And in art generally, in all the arts, we find the same sort of unarguable preconceived false opinion, the same sort of aberration. Our period is offering us the spectacle of a coherence in moral absurdity. But just because of this very coherence, we are forced to assert without a shadow of hesitation that this cult of the morally absurd is very rapidly becoming a cult of the positively evil.

On the nature of evil, in this book, underlying the more detailed arguments, there is a sort of meditation of mine; a meditation which has so far arrived only at very general results, and with which I am very far from being satisfied myself. Evil is a mystery; it is not something which can be assimilated to the notion of something lacking, even to the sort of lack which is a deformity. On this point I should be tempted to say, very broadly, that the gnostics, from Jacob Boehme to Schelling and Berdyaev, are right: here again the rationalizing philosophers have been led away by the spirit of abstraction.

But this word 'mystery' is not a simple signboard placed at the entrance to a straight path. The reflections which follow all imply, I think, that mystery is coextensive with what I should like to call (on the analogy of the metaphysical) the *metatechnical*: by which term I merely intend to mark off roughly that infrangible sphere of being to which techniques are never able to gain access. In Great Britain, neo-positivistic philosophies have been making alarming inroads lately, and it was partly for that reason that I found myself making to a student audience there observations to the following effect: 'Calculating machines rightly astonish us, and for my own part I am quite incapable of saying to what degree of perfection they may be brought. But what we can quite certainly affirm is that it will never be possible to construct a machine capable of *interrogating itself* on the conditions that make it possible and on the limits of its own range of operations . . .'These remarks were an illustration of that notion of an intimate link between reflection and mystery which lies at the foundation of all my work. Yet we are forced to admit that the more techniques advance, the more reflection is thrust into the background—and I believe that this cannot be a matter of mere chance. Not, for that matter, that I should like to assert that there is anything necessarily fated, or fatal, about the connection; but what does seem certain is that the progress and above all the extreme diffusion of techniques tends to create a spiritual and intellectual atmosphere (or more precisely, an anti-spiritual and anti-intellectual atmosphere) as unfavourable as possible to the exercise of reflection; and this observation may prepare us to understand why to-day the idea of the universal can be affirmed only outside the mass world and against that world.

The universal against the masses: no doubt that should really be the title of this book. But what *is* the universal? What are we to understand by it? Not, of course, it goes without saying, a wretched abstract truth reducible to formulas that could be handed down and learned by rote. The universal is spirit or mind—and spirit or mind is love. On this point, as on so many others, we have to go back to Plato. Not, of course, to the mere letter of a philosophy of which, for that matter, hardly more than the letter, than the outward, unsecret aspect, has come down to us—but to the essential message which that philosophy still has for us to-day. Between love and intelligence, there can be no real divorce. Such a divorce is apparently consummated only when intelligence is degraded or, if I may be allowed the expression, becomes merely cerebral; and, of course, when love reduces itself to mere carnal appetite. But this we must assert, and as forcibly as possible: where love on one side, where intelligence on the other, reach their highest expression, they cannot fail to meet: do not let us speak of their becoming identical, for there can be no mutual identity except between abstractions;

intelligence and love are the most concrete things in the world, and at a certain level every great thinker has recognized this or had a presentiment of it.

But in point of fact the masses exist and develop (following laws which are fundamentally purely mechanical) only at a level far below that at which intelligence and love are possible. Why should this be so? Because the masses partake of the human only in a degraded state, they are themselves a degraded state of the human. Do not let us seek to persuade ourselves that an education of the masses is possible: that is a contradiction in terms. What is educable is only an individual, or more exactly a person. Everywhere else, there is no scope for anything but a *training*. Let us say rather that what we have to do is to introduce a social and political order which will withdraw the greatest number of beings possible from this mass state of abasement or alienation. One mark of that state is that the masses are of their very essence—I repeat, *of their very essence*—the stuff of which fanaticism is made: propaganda has on them the convulsive effect of an electrical shock. It arouses them not to life, but to that appearance of life which particularly manifests itself in riots and revolutions. Also, of course, it is usual—and I do not know that the essential principle of this necessity has ever been grasped—on such occasions for the very dregs of the population to rise to the surface and take command of events. It is at the lowest level that the crystallization of mass impulses to violences takes place. Yet this is not to say that, if revolutions are bad in themselves, they are without some element of counterbalancing good; they might be compared to certain crises in the development of a living organism, which are pathological in themselves, but which seem to be needed to secure, in a very risky fashion, the future growth of that organism by snatching it from torpor and death.

At the end of this book, it will be my duty to indicate some of the more positive conclusions to which such reflections on the antagonism between the universal and the masses ought to lead us.

CHAPTER I

WHAT IS A FREE MAN?

A PROBLEM such as the one we are dealing with in this chapter, 'What is a free man?' cannot, or so it seems to me, be usefully discussed in the abstract. It cannot be discussed, that is, out of the context of historical situations, considered in their concrete fullness; it is, for that matter, of the very essence of the human lot that man always is in a situation of some sort or other, and this is what a too abstract kind of humanism always runs the risk of forgetting. We are not therefore here asking ourselves what a free man is *in se*, what the essential notion of a free man is; for that question very possibly has no meaning at all. But we are asking ourselves how in an historical situation which is *our* situation, which we have to face here and now, man's freedom can be conceived, and how we can bear witness to it.

About seventy-five years ago, Nietzsche asserted: 'God is dead'. To-day, we can hear, not so much boldly asserted as muttered in anguish, a statement that seems to echo that of Nietzsche: 'Man is in his death-throes'. Let us make ourselves clear; this statement, by those who make it sincerely, is not intended to have the force of prophecy; at the level of reflective awareness (and it is at this level that the statement is made) we cannot make any sort of pronouncement at all on coming events, we are in fact even forced to acknowledge our ignorance of the future. And there is a sense in which we ought even to rejoice in that ignorance, for it is that ignorance alone which makes possible that perpetual hopeful betting on the future without which human activity, as such, would find itself radically inhibited. To say that man is in his death-throes is only to say that man to-day finds himself facing, not some external event, such as the annihilation of our planet, for instance, which might be the consequence of some catastrophe in the heavens, but rather possibilities of complete self-destruction inherent in himself. These possibilities, always latent, become patent from the moment in which man makes a bad use, or rather an impious use, of the powers that constitute his nature. I am thinking here both of the atomic bomb and of techniques of human degradation, as these have been put into effect in all totalitarian states without exception. Between the physical destruction wrought by the atomic bomb and the spiritual destruction wrought by techniques of human degradation there exists, quite certainly, a secret bond; it is precisely the duty of reflective thinking to lay bare that secret.

The relationship which can exist between the two statements, 'God is dead', 'Man is in his death-throes', is not only a complex relationship, but an ambiguous one. We can ask ourselves, for instance, whether Nietzsche's cry of exultation or pain did not, just like the modern cry of mere pain, presuppose a concrete historical situation; linked itself, like our situation, to a preliminary misuse of human powers, of which men at that time had been guilty. No doubt we ought to recognize that the relationship between the two statements, 'God is dead', and 'Man is in his death-throes', is concrete and existential, not logical: it is quite impossible to extract from Nietzsche's statement about God by any method of analysis the other statement about man, though Nietzsche perhaps would have accepted the statement about man, at least during the ultimate or penultimate period of his working life. Even if he had accepted it, however, he would probably not have perceived all the overtones in the statement, 'Man is in his death-throes', which we can perceive to-day. Also (this is a strange reflection, but a true one) it is perhaps by starting from the statement, 'Man is in his death-throes', that we may be able to question once more the statement, 'God is dead', and to discover that God is living after all. It is, as the reader will soon discover, towards the latter conclusion that the whole of my subsequent argument tends.

But what we have to ask ourselves first is the following question: what becomes of freedom in a world in which man, or at least man at a certain level of self-awareness, is forced to recognize that he has entered into his death-throes?

At this point, however, we may be faced with a preliminary objection. It is one which presents itself readily to the mind. Might it not be convenient to say that the question, 'What is a free man?' can only receive a positive answer in a country which has itself remained a free country?

However, the very notion of a free country or a free people, on a little analysis, appears to be a much less distinct notion than we should be tempted to think it at first. I shall take two examples: Switzerland, as the sequel to a process of political blackmail, found itself under the necessity of putting its factories to work for the benefit of Nazi Germany—was Switzerland still a free country? Sweden, at the end of the war, was obliged to conclude with Soviet Russia a very burdensome trade treaty, which had the effect of throttling her economic life. Ought not Sweden to have admitted to herself that—at the level of facts, if not at the level of words—she was no longer a free country? If the freedom of a people or a country be defined as *absolute independence*, is it not obvious that in a world like ours freedom cannot exist, not only because of inevitable economic interdependences, but because of the part played by pressure, or, less politely, by blackmail, at all levels of international intercourse?

Following out this line of thought, we should be led to acknowledge that the individual himself, in any country whatsoever, not only finds himself dependent but finds himself, in a great many cases, obliged to carry out actions which his conscience disapproves. (We have only to think, for instance, of military conscription and its consequences to become aware of this fact.) All that we can say is that in countries where there is still a recognition of what we can call in a very general fashion the rights of the human person, a certain number of guarantees of freedom survive: but we ought immediately to add that such guarantees are becoming less and less numerous and that, failing a very improbable reversal of the present general tendency of things, there will be a continuing demand for their further reduction. It would be contrary to the facts of the case to assert that men, in what we broadly call 'the free countries', enjoy absolute independence.

That does not matter so much, for, except to a pedantic type of anarchist, such absolute independence is inconceivable. But it would also be contrary to the facts to assert that men in free countries to-day generally possess the power to square their conduct with their consciences.

This is the point at which we ought to pass to the extreme case and ask ourselves what becomes of the freedom of the individual, even of what we call his inner freedom, in a totalitarian country. Here, I believe, we shall find ourselves forced to recognize an exceptionally important fact: Stoicism (and I am thinking less of an abstract philosophical doctrine than of a spiritual attitude) has been to-day, I shall not say refuted by the facts, but uprooted by them from the soil which used to nourish it. This ancient and respectable attitude rested on the distinction made so forcibly and severely by such writers as Epictetus, Seneca, and Marcus Aurelius: the distinction between what depends on my will, and what does not depend on it. Stoic thought, in so far as it was not merely formulated in abstract terms but adopted with dauntless courage as a way of life, implied a belief in the inner tribunal of conscience: a tribunal unviolated, and indeed inviolable, by any intrusion of external power. There can be no Stoicism without a belief in an inalienable inner sovereignty, an absolute possession of the self by the self.

However, the very essence of those modern techniques of degradation, to which I made an earlier allusion, consists precisely in putting the individual into a situation in which he loses touch with himself, in which he is literally beside himself, even to the point of being able sincerely to disavow acts into which nevertheless he had put sincerely his whole heart, or on the other hand of being able to confess to acts which he had not committed. I shall not attempt at this point to define the *kind* of sincerity, obviously a factitious and artificial kind, that we are talking of. I shall note merely that, though in recent years such techniques of degradation have been brought to an almost unimaginable degree of refinement, they were already in use in periods much earlier than ours. I was told recently that during the trial of the Knights Templars under Philip the Fair confessions were obtained by processes which cannot have consisted merely of physical torture; since later on, during a second and last retractation of their original confessions, the accused, once more in possession of their faculties, declared that they had originally *sincerely* accused themselves of acts which they *had not committed*. Physical torture by itself seems incapable of producing such sincerity; it can be evoked only by those abominable methods of *psychological* manipulation to which so many countries, in such various latitudes, have in recent years had recourse.

Given these conditions, the situation that each one of us must face to-day is as follows: (I say *each one of us*, supposing that we do not want to lie to ourselves or to commit the sin of unwarranted presumption; given that supposition, we must admit that there are real and practical methods that can be applied to any of us to-morrow with the effect of depriving us of self-sovereignty or, less grandiosely, of self-control: even though in another age we should have had sound reasons for regarding that self-sovereignty as infrangible and inviolable). Our situation, then, is this: we ought not even to say, as the Stoics said, that even at the very worst there remains for us the possibility of suicide, as a happy way out. That is no longer a true statement of the case. A man to-day can be put into a situation in which he *will no longer want to kill himself*; in which suicide will appear to him as an *illicit* or *unfair* way out; in which he will think of himself as under an obligation not merely to suffer, but to wish for, the punishment appropriate to crimes which he will impute to himself *without having committed them*.

It may be objected here that the mere mention of such horrible possibilities is itself dangerous, almost criminal. Certainly, if I were addressing myself to a class of schoolboys or students, it might be proper to leave this aspect of my subject in the shadow. But I am addressing myself to mature minds, minds I assume already capable of higher reflection; and on such minds, just because of their maturity, a real responsibility rests.

What we have to recognize is this. Thanks to the techniques of degradation it is creating and perfecting, a materialistic mode of thought, in our time, is showing itself capable of bringing into being a world which more and more *tends to verify its own materialistic postulates.* I mean that a human being who has undergone a certain type of psychological manipulation tends progressively to be reduced to the status of a mere *thing*; a psychic thing, of course, but nevertheless a thing which falls quite tidily within the province of the theories elaborated by an essentially materialistic psychology. This assertion of mine is, of course, obviously ambiguous; it does not mean that this materialistic psychology, with however startling powers of reductive transformation it may become endowed, will ever be of a nature to grasp and reveal to us reality as it is in itself. Rather, my assertion emphasizes the fact that there is nothing surprising for a philosophy like my own, a philosophy of man as a being in a situation, in the fact that man depends, to a very great degree, on the idea he has of himself and that this idea cannot be degraded without at the same time degrading man. This is one more reason, and on the face of things the most serious and imperative reason, for condemning materialistic thinking, root and branch. And it is relevant to note here that in our day the materialistic attitude has acquired a virulence and a cohesion which it was far from possessing in the last century. It was a common spectacle then to see thinkers who regarded themselves as thoroughly imbued with materialistic principles showing in their personal lives all the scrupulosity of Kantian rigorists.

It may seem that I am rather straying here from the question which I set out to answer at the beginning of this chapter, 'What is a free man?' But this is not in fact by any means the case, for it is very important for us to recognize, whatever fancies certain thinkers incapable of the least coherence may have had about this question, that a materialistic conception of the universe is radically incompatible with the idea of a free man: more precisely, that, in a society ruled by materialistic principles, freedom is transmuted into its opposite, or becomes merely the most treacherous and deceptive of empty slogans.

Theoretically, of course, we can imagine the possibility of man's preserving a minimum of independence even in a society ruled on materialistic principles; but, as we ought to be immediately aware, this possibility is an evanescent one, implying contradictions: for freedom in such a society would consist, if I may put it so, in rendering oneself sufficiently insignificant to escape the attention of the men in power. But is it not fairly obvious that this wish for insignificance, supposing even that it is a wish that can be put into effect, is already in a sense a suicidal wish? In such a society, the mere keeping, for instance, of an intimate diary might be a capital crime, and one does not see why, by the use of tape recorders and tapped telephones, as well as by various quite conceivable extensions of the use of radio, it should not be quite possible to keep the police well informed about the thoughts and the feelings of any individual whatsoever*. From the point of view of the individual in such a society, there is no conceivable way out at all: private life, as such, does not exist any more.

But let us imagine, then, the situation of our own country immediately after a *putsch* or a *coup d'état:* if rebellion is futile, and a retreat into insignificance impracticable, what, supposing that we are fully aware of our situation, does there remain for us to do? At the risk of discontenting and even of shocking those who still tend to think of solutions for political problems in terms of positive action, I shall say that in that region all the ways of escape seem to me to be barred. Our only recourse can be to the Transcendent: but what does that mean? 'The transcendent', 'transcendence', these are words which among philosophers and intellectuals, for a good many years past, have been strangely misused. When I myself speak here of a recourse to the transcendent, I mean, as concretely as possible, that our only chance in the sort of horrible situation I have imagined is to appeal, I should perhaps *not* say to a power, but rather to a level of being, an order of the spirit, which is also the level and order of grace, of mercy, of charity; and to proclaim, while there is still time, that is to say before the state's psychological manipulations have produced in us the alienation from our true selves that we fear, that we repudiate *in advance* the deeds and the acts that may be obtained from us by any sort of constraint whatsoever. We solemnly affirm, by this

*See George Orwell's *1984*.

appeal to the transcendent, that the reality of our selves lies *beyond* any such acts and any such words. It will be said, no doubt, that by this gesture we are giving ourselves a very ideal, a very unreal, sort of satisfaction; but to say so is to fail to recognize the real nature of the thought which I am groping to put into shape. What we have to do is to proclaim that we do *not* belong entirely to the world of objects to which men are seeking to assimilate us, in which they are straining to imprison us. To put it very concretely indeed, we have to proclaim that this life of ours, which it has now become technically possible to make into a hideous and grimacing parody of all our dreams, may in reality be only the most insignificant aspect of a grand process unfolding itself far beyond the boundaries of the visible world. In other words, this amounts to saying that *all philosophies of immanence have had their day*, that in our own day they have revealed their basic unreality or, what is infinitely more serious, their complicity with those modern idolatries which it is our duty to denounce without pity: the idolatry of race, the idolatry of class. I should add here that even the authentic religions may become similarly degraded in their very principle of being. They too can degenerate into idolatries; especially where the will to power is waiting to corrupt them; and this, alas, is almost invariably the case when the Church becomes endowed with temporal authority.

But we are now on the road towards a number of pretty positive conclusions. I should formulate them as follows: a man cannot be free or remain free, except in the degree to which he remains linked with that which transcends him, whatever the particular form of that link may be: for it is pretty obvious that the form of the link need not reduce itself to official and canonical prayers. I should say that in the case particularly of the true artist in paint, or stone, or music, or words, this relationship to the transcendent is something that is experienced in the most authentic and profound way. I am supposing, of course, that he does not yield to the innumerable temptations to which the artist is exposed to-day: the temptation to startle, to innovate at all costs, to shut oneself up in a private world leaving as few channels as possible open for communication with the world of eternal forms: and so on. But nothing could be falser and more dangerous than to base on these observations of mine some sort of neo-aestheticism. We have to recognize that there are modes of creation which do not belong to the aesthetic order, and which are within the reach of everybody; and it is in so far as he is a creator, at however humble a level, that any man at all can recognize his own freedom. It would be necessary, moreover, to show that the idea of being creative, taken in this quite general sense, always implies the idea of being open towards others: that openness I have called in my Gifford Lectures, intersubjectivity, whether that is conceived as *agape* (charity) or *philia* (attachment): these two notions, in any case, I think, tend ultimately to converge. But what must be stated as forcibly as possible is that societies built on a materialistic basis, whatever place they tactfully leave for a collective and at bottom purely animal exaltation, sin radically against intersubjectivity; they exclude it in principle; and it is because they exclude it, that they grub up every possible freedom by its roots.

It is quite conceivable—and I put this idea forward not as an abstract hypothesis but as a familiar fact—that in a country enslaved by a totalitarian power, a man might find himself constrained, not merely in order to live but in order to withdraw his dependants from a state of absolute wretchedness, to accept, for instance, a job with the security police: a job which might compel him to carry out acts absolutely repugnant to his conscience. Is mere refusal to carry out such acts a solution to his problem? We may doubt this, for the very reason that such a refusal might entail direful consequences not only for the man himself but for his innocent dependants. But it could happen that the man who accepted such a job might make a religious vow to use the share of power which he has been given so much as possible to help the very people of whom he was officially the persecutor. Such a vow, with the creative power that it re-bestows on him who makes it, is a concrete example of that recourse to the transcendent of which I spoke earlier on. But it is obvious that there is nothing in such an extremely particular case out of which any general rule can be framed. A rigoristic moral formalism, an attempt to bring all human acts under very general rules, ceases almost entirely to be acceptable as soon as one becomes aware of that element of the unique and the incommensurable which is the portion of every concrete being, confronted with a concrete situation. No two beings, and no two situations, are really commensurable with each other. To become aware of this fact is to undergo a sort of crisis. But it is with this crisis in our moral awareness as a starting-point, that there becomes possible that cry from us towards the creative principle, and that demand by it on us, which each must answer in his own way, if he does not wish to become an accomplice of what Simone Weil called 'the gross beast'. In our world as it is to-day there can be hardly any set of circumstances in which we may not be forced to ask ourselves whether, through our free choice, through our particular decisions, we are not going to make ourselves guilty of just such a complicity.

CHAPTER II

LOST LIBERTIES

THERE are lost liberties—and those among the most precious—which we can never reasonably hope to regain. Let me be more precise: the parties in power, who imagine rightly or wrongly that they are leading France along the paths of 'progress', think that many of these lost liberties, in so far as they were open to abuse, or were balanced on the other side by indefensible social inequalities, ought to be given up for good and all, as corresponding to a stage of social organization (or rather, disorganization) which we have now happily left behind us. From this point of view, the limitations and controls of all kinds which we come up against when we want to dispose freely of our property, for instance, or to form certain kinds of association, will be regarded as the expression in these spheres—a negative expression from our selfish point of view, but in reality, or from society's point of view, a positive one—of progressive social tendencies with which the powers that be are perfectly ready to force us to comply, if by any chance we are not ready to co-operate wholeheartedly with these tendencies of our own free will.

There is a preliminary observation to be made here; it is that in relation to this topic two kinds of quite distinct, and not necessarily compatible, considerations are relevant.

One of these considerations is equality: the illegitimate kinds of liberty, of which it is the general intention to deprive us, are regarded as intolerable privileges which have to be reduced and finally suppressed, till the situation of each of us becomes as similar as possible to that of his neighbour.

The other consideration is social organization: kinds of freedom that are thought of as archaic are looked at less in themselves than in their social effects. There is a danger of these social effects tending towards anarchy and thus hampering a rational social organization which men claim to-day to be bringing into being.

But it is glaringly obvious that we cannot make any absolute *a priori* pronouncement about the degree of equality or inequality that is implied by, or more exactly, that can be tolerated by, an ideal degree of social organization; or, in more exact language, that will allow for the most plentiful output in some definite sphere of production. We have heard, often enough, that in Soviet Russia to-day for instance, there is a more striking inequality of salaries and wages than is to be found anywhere else; and it is obvious that it is precisely in the name of organization and output that this inequality has been allowed to increase so considerably. In a country like France, however, even sympathizers with Soviet Russia pretend to base themselves on the postulate that a high degree of economic equality and a high economic output go together; but nobody is any longer deceived by this attitude, which is maintained for merely tactical reasons of a sort very easy to discover.

It is clear, however, that in the long run considerations of organization and output must of necessity prevail; even if this should only happen after some shocking crisis. For, if a country were to cease to interest itself in output, it would be, by an almost fatal necessity, reduced to a servile condition by countries that had sacrificed everything to output—whether or not this reduction to a servile condition were carried out by ostensibly peaceful means; between peaceful and warlike means of subjugation, for that matter, the distinction in the extreme cases on either side is rapidly vanishing away.

But what we ought to insist on is that at the present moment, in France, for instance, this sinister ambiguity in the popular argument for equality—that those who demand the greatest equality claim to be thinking of the nation's economic strength, when in fact they may be secretly encouraging its weakness—has not really been cleared away: and that levelling down, that is to say the basest and easiest way of seeking social equality, is the principle which seems to underly most of the legal arrangements which in France weigh so heavily on our day-to-day existence.

The kind of equality thus brought into being has one purpose alone, that of disguising from those who apparently benefit from it the system of oppressive administrative rule to which they are being condemned.

Who *seem* to benefit from it, I say: for who really benefits? Where does the real benefit lie? It is not a material benefit. It is an imaginary and sentimental one, and the fantasies and sentiments to which it appeals are of the basest sort: the satisfaction which this kind of equality affords me is the opportunity of feeling, if I am exposed to constraints and vexations, or am in an actual state of wretchedness, that my neighbour is in the same boat. A very negative satisfaction, it will be said. But perhaps not so negative as all that, after all: it is in fact—as Nietzsche and Scheler have seen, and have shown with wonderful clearness—the satisfaction of an aspiration whose basis lies in the resentment felt by man against his neighbour. This satisfaction, in fact, is the most degraded, the most perverted shape that can be taken by the interest that a man always has in his neighbour: it is a wretched and perverted substitute for that love of one's neighbour as oneself of which the Gospels speak.

At the moment, what we have to show is that this feeling of resentment against one's neighbour tends to develop step by step with the increasing importance of the administrative function in the world: that is to say, with the multiplication of parasitical and purely functionary activities which are not only not creative, but which are destined to cripple and finally to paralyse every possible sort of really creative activity. Such a situation becomes inevitable as soon as activities consisting essentially of control and restraint begin to gain the day over activities which have to be controlled and restrained. It is in this field that resentment can make its choices; and the reason for this is pretty obvious; it is that it becomes less and less possible, except at the high levels, for somebody employed in a great administrative machine to take a real interest in what he is doing, that is, in a task as abstract and impersonal as possible, on which the individual, almost by the nature of the case, can leave no mark of his own. In the long run, what can the law of work for the minor civil servant be except to do as little as possible; in fact, to do nothing more than is needed in order not to draw attention to himself, and so risk losing his job or rather his 'post'. From the moment in which my own job, which I nevertheless do not want to lose, ceases to interest me, my interest will tend to be obliquely directed towards the other man's job. And in the other man and his job, I shall hardly see, as in Sartre's world, anything more than a threat to myself; the other man, for me, becomes the person who covets my job, or, more subtly, who damages my inner esteem because he manages to get a better-paid job than mine. In all this, there is a merciless logic which, of course, one imagines that a certain number of functionaries can resist, but only to the degree in which they are still given grace to do so or are affected by some of the remoter workings of grace. For, as I think one can never insist too forcibly, individual goodness is inconceivable without grace. It is therefore, on the whole, inconceivable that this destructive resentment should not tend to spread itself quite generally about the administrative world like an infectious disease: it is a sort of moral blood-poisoning. The only natural end to such a process is military or economic catastrophe; such catastrophes occur at the moment when a society whose constitution has insensibly degenerated becomes absolutely paralytic; it collapses.

But it is all too obvious that it is not through such catastrophes that our lost liberties will find the chance to reassert themselves; all we can say is that at such moments the veil of appearances, by which our consciences still wish to be deceived, is rent from top to bottom, and the reality of our situation is revealed in all its nakedness. But let us suppose that the catastrophe of which we are thinking does not entail the subjugation of a country by some foreign power, working within it, for a longer or shorter time, like a malignant growth; let us suppose that by some unhoped-for chance the recovery of the country still remains possible. That recovery will be brought about only by the acceptance of an even more severe administrative regulation of daily life. It would really be of very little interest at this moment to digress into prognostications about the condition of France in coming years. On the other hand, it is important that we ask ourselves what is the basis of, and how we have been able to bring about, the sort of general anaesthesia thanks to which the French, a short while ago so easily frightened by any threat at all to their liberties, have been able to endure the spectacle of the amputation of their fundamental freedoms. *To endure the spectacle*, I say: but what is probable is that my noun here is inappropriate, and that the operation has been carried out in conditions under which the patient was unaware of what was happening to him. Such, at least, is one's broad sense of the matter.

For, in the first place, this amputation of our freedoms was carried out at a time when the attention of the man in the street was almost exclusively concentrated on the problem of earning his daily bread and on the exhausting difficulties which he had to confront merely in order to remain alive. Our key notion here is that of insecurity. In a state of radical insecurity, and moreover in a world-wide state of such insecurity, the preoccupation of the individual is to find any prop at all to lean on, and the general movement which has impelled so many Frenchmen to seek posts in the Civil Service needs no other explanation: the State, after the war, was considered as the sole dispenser of that security, those guarantees, which men formerly sought for in religion or in their daily productive work—when that could be carried out, that is, in morally and physically healthy conditions: that is to say, in the far away times when the artisan could still have something of the craftsman's pride in his work and sense of independence. Nobody, I think, would dream of denying that this mass movement towards State employment is in the nature of a sort of mad rush towards servitude; even though in our own transitional period, such servitude still tends to deceive itself about what it essentially is.

We ought to emphasize at this point certain parallel considerations. In particular we ought to show how the growth of partisan political hatreds has helped, in France, to erase our feeling for our fundamental liberties. It is relevant here to allude to the continuing scandal, which we in France have had to witness since the beginning of the purge; and to the incredible apathy of public opinion in the face of this scandal. To be sure, we ought to make considerable allowances for the general social phenomenon of habituation to the shocking. There does come a moment when public sensibility simply ceases to react. But this phenomenon is a notably complex one: how could it come about, for instance, that the same men who had fought and suffered to deliver their country from the Gestapo should, once they had attained power, have either brought into being or at least tolerated methods of persecution which were not essentially different from those under which they had themselves suffered? Here, we should think not so much of acquiring a habit as of being infected by a contagion. As soon as certain methods of persecution are put into effect anywhere at all, they tend automatically to be put into effect quite generally. What we ought therefore rather to do is to look into the rather exceptional, and basically paradoxical, cases of the few countries where this contagion did not operate; or rather, where public opinion reacted vigorously against a clearly perceived danger. I am thinking of Holland and Belgium rather than Great Britain. Great Britain was spared the Nazi occupation, and partisan political passions there were very far from reaching the state of paroxysm which was so common in countries that felt the direct weight of Nazi oppression. It is much more relevant in this connection to compare what happened in France after the war with what happened in Holland, where, so far as one can judge, the sense of freedom has not so far been seriously affected by the events of the war years. In preserving a spirit of sanity in Holland, the strong continuing religious sentiment of the Dutch, the smallness of their territory, giving every man an intimate feeling for his country as a whole, and their attachment to their Royal Family, have obviously played a major part. One should add that the fact that there was not interposed between the Dutch people and their oppressors a puppet government, like that of Pétain, spared Holland certain evils from which we in France continue to suffer. The lie of

Vichy undoubtedly paved the way for the lies of the Resistance. Thus there was brought about in France an essentially unhealthy national situation, which of its very nature—as is always the case with such situations—could hardly fail to work against our liberties. For it cannot be too forcibly affirmed that lies, from whatever source they emanate, always work in favour of servitude. Between the acceptance of lies and the loss of liberties there is a connection none the less real for not being obvious; and it is a connection which those charged with the interests of France should become aware of. I know, of course, that the thinking of men with heavy practical responsibilities tends to become thin and poor; that, in fact, may be a fatality inherent in democracy's very nature (if this phrase, for that matter, has any real meaning); but it is a deficiency, this deficiency of creative thought at the highest governmental levels, from which France in particular has suffered for many years.

There can be no question here of putting forward any simple and easy remedies for evils which are so deeply rooted in our whole national life. All we can assert, on the one hand, and without hesitation, is that our present political system in France can merely with increasing rapidity aggravate these evils; and on the other hand, that it would be both silly and criminal to place any hopes in a neo-Fascism, of which, after our experiences during the war years, the mere thought ought to fill us with horror. But in fact, failing some quite general conflagration which would change the face of things altogether, France seems to have no practical choice to-day except between a Communist system, which would in fact be probably merely an aggravated Fascism and would believe it was solving problems merely by eliminating the given factors in national life and tradition from which these problems spring, and a monarchical system, in accordance with the oldest traditions of our country, but of which the very idea, it must be admitted, is inconceivable to most Frenchmen to-day: to be a living, practical, working system, moreover, a French monarchy would have to adapt itself to economic and even psychological conditions which have no relation at all to the conditions of monarchical France in the past.

It is more to the point at the moment to note the general characteristics of the kind of internal reformation (and by that, I mean, above all, spiritual reformation) which alone could pave the way for the advent of such a monarchical system. This work of reformation, in which each one of us in France is bound to lend a hand, in however humble a sphere his light may shine, consists above all in a restoration of values; we have to learn to grasp once more the distinction between the true and the false, the good and the evil, the just and the unjust—slowly and painfully, just as a paralytic who has recovered the use of his limbs learns slowly and painfully once more how to walk. What we are talking of here is a process of national re-education which, even at the very moment in which we pledge ourselves to it, seems almost unrealizable and even almost impossible to conceive. Nevertheless, the illusion which we must quite pitilessly proscribe is that the very word freedom can retain any meaning at all after the sense of human values has disappeared; and by the sense of values we must also understand the feeling that values are transcendent. One might say without any paradox at all that what men need most at the present hour is a course of treatment according to the prescriptions of Plato.

CHAPTER III

TECHNIQUES OF DEGRADATION

It can never be too strongly emphasized that the crisis which Western man is undergoing to-day is a metaphysical one; there is probably no more dangerous illusion than that of imagining that some readjustment of social or institutional conditions could suffice of itself to appease a contemporary sense of disquiet which rises, in fact, from the very depths of man's being.

This does not, of course, imply that the existence of such a crisis at the metaphysical level can be legitimately used as an argument by men of conservative, or sometimes of Machiavellian, temperament, to justify their own inertia at the social level, their strong reluctance, for instance, to carry out reforms which before the war were long overdue, and which at that time could have been effected, at least in France, in much less burdensome conditions than they can to-day. But this observation is foreign to my main purpose in this chapter; and if I have nevertheless made it, it is in order to parry in advance the political interpretation which certain readers will be tempted to give of all the remarks that follow. To-day, unfortunately, there is a danger of political preoccupations falsifying all discussions, all honest attempts at analysis.

Speaking in the most general fashion, I do think that after the terrible events which have been devastating our human world it is absolutely necessary to draw up some sort of human balance sheet. With this purpose in mind, we should put to the best use the sort of uneasy truce which is now all that is left to us; a truce for that matter which perhaps cannot be maintained for very long. However short it is, it does seem that it may be long enough to set free that faculty of forgetfulness which, in every realm of human activity, seems to work with such disconcerting speed. On this matter, as on so many others, Péguy grasped the essentials and expressed them with incomparable energy. Let us recall, for instance, the famous passage from his *Clio:* 'History consists essentially of passing *along the line* of an event, of reviewing an event. Memory consists essentially of being *within* the event, of above all not emerging *from* the event; in remaining there and going over it again from within . . . History is the elderly general, plastered with medals, brisk and impotent, who reviews the long lines of troops, laden with their heavy field-kit, on the barrack-square of some garrison town'. But this is just to say that in a very deep sense history itself is also *a way of forgetting*, or, to put it more flatly, of losing that real contact with the event for the lack of which historical narrative so often reduces itself to a simple abstracting *naming* of events. We are often astonished at the extraordinary unreadiness men show to learn from the lessons of the past. Paradoxical though this may be, I think that history in its modern form, and especially in so far as it tends to oppose itself more and more to that kind of popular tradition which is still a living memory and a store-house of the past, has a great share of responsibility for this sad state of affairs. The past, when it is merely known historically (that is, as a subject for abstract study), somehow piles itself up outside our real lives; or it is fated to lose what one might be tempted to call its vitamins. To be sure, there do exist, apart from and outside the history which is worked up by historians, direct personal eyewitness accounts of great events of the past which have quite another quality; but almost of necessity there does come a moment in which such old diaries, letters, or memoirs begin to be read rather as we read novels; in which they annex themselves somehow to that indeterminate world of prose fiction which has such obscure, fantastic, and deceptive relations with the world of real activity.

I think that one of the duties of a philosopher, if he shows himself worthy of his vocation to-day, is to attack quite directly those dissimulating forces which are all working towards what might be called the neutralization of the past; and whose conjoint effect consists in arousing in contemporary man a feeling of what I should like to call insulation in time. In this realm as in many others, I think we ought to aim at a restoration of that unity of poetic vision and philosophic creativity of which the great pre-Socratic philosophers offer us one of the first known examples. It is not a matter of mere chance if it is in the work of a writer like Péguy or Valéry—the Valéry of *Regards sur le Monde actuel*—as sometimes also, though much more infrequently, in the work of a writer like Claudel, that we find these sudden lightning-flashes of penetration into human reality which the conscientious professional historian and the specialist philosopher to-day seem condemned to miss: exactly as one misses a promotion, or a train.

Some readers may object that the sort of human balance-sheet which I have in mind, if it is to have an objective value, presupposes a remote detachment, from which contemporaries of the man who draws it up, still themselves immersed in the struggle, will not be able to benefit. I think that this is a complete mistake, and that when people talk of drawing back from life to see it in perspective they are letting themselves be deceived by metaphors from optics which, in this realm of discourse, have no valid application. I am not sure that a serious writer ought still to speak at all of 'existentialism'; for, day by day, in a certain kind of newspaper in France, this word is put to quite thoughtless uses. But we ought perhaps to say that the merit of existentialist philosophy, in so far as we can properly speak of such a thing at all, consists more than anything else in transcending and rejecting the mode of thought which has become incarnate in optical metaphors. It is probably, in fact, quite untrue to suppose that there exists for a given historical event the moral equivalent of that point in space at which we might be recommended to place ourselves to get the most clear, distinct, and satisfying view of some physical object. At first, this may seem another paradox: will not years, for instance, have to elapse before we can gather together the necessary documents to give an exact account of what happened in France during the Occupation? Yes: but we still have to know whether this exhaustive documentation, which makes such a complete account of events possible, is not likely in its own way to blind us, too: or in other words whether the warmth of the living event must not have dissipated itself before the historian can perform his dissection? Of course, I am myself the first to acknowledge that I am dealing here with a dark and complex problem. All that we should insist on, I think, is that an event in time is not comparable to an object in space, and that those who claim to reconstitute integrally a past series of events always run the risk of substituting for it something which is not it, perhaps something chimerical. Given these conditions, is it not one of the duties of the philosopher, or more precisely of the philosopher-poet, to endeavour to snatch, if I may put it so, that *soul* of the event, which the historian, if he for his part is not a poet—and historians to-day seem less and less to recognize that they have a right to be poets if they want to—is on the other hand almost fatally condemned to allow to escape from him: to allow to escape just on account of these objective precautions which he is forced to take to safeguard his illusory reconstitution of the past.

It is in this spirit, at least, that I wish now to get to grips with my reflections on contemporary techniques of human degradation, and to attempt to mark connections that are not always immediately perceptible between certain orders of event which are more usually considered separately.

It is obvious that as soon as one begins to speak of techniques of degradation, one cannot help calling up for the reader in the first place the notion of the massive and systematic employment of such techniques with which the Nazis made us familiar, particularly in their concentration camps. Perhaps it might be useful here to make a sort of preliminary attempt at definition: in a restricted sense, I understand by 'techniques of degradation' a whole body of methods deliberately put into operation in order to attack and destroy in human persons belonging to some definite class or other their self-respect, and in order to transform them little by little into mere human waste products, conscious of themselves as such, and in the end forced to despair of themselves, not merely at an intellectual level, but in the very depths of their souls. On this point, of course, there is an abundance of direct eye-witness accounts, and we can disregard legends like that of the dog-man of Buchenwald. I will confine myself to quoting two or three passages which seem to me, on this topic, to be quite revealing enough.

'The Germans', writes Madame Jacqueline Richet about Ravensbruck, 'sought by every conceivable means to degrade us. They exploited every kind of cowardice, they excited every kind of jealousy and stimulated and encouraged every kind of hate. One had to make a daily effort to sustain one's moral integrity. The veneer of civilization soon rubs away, and one sees that society ladies are not the last among us to start behaving like fishwives. But what is much more serious is the sordid expedients to which the weaker among us are ready to lower themselves. A good education, a good background does not always act as a moral support, and one witnesses daily shocking moral collapses under the pressure of hunger . . . I have seen women willingly become domestic servants of *Aufseherinnen*, of *Blocovas* or of ward commandants. I have seen others laughing at the brutalities of S.S. guards in order to avoid being struck themselves. I have heard of spying and tale-bearing which, especially in the workshops, makes life impossible'. (*Trois Bagnes*, pp. 128–129).

After having given frightful details about the mis-management of the huts at Auschwitz, Madame Lewinska writes as follows: 'And now I understood. I understood that it was not a matter of disorder or lack of organization, but that on the contrary it was a mature and conscious principle which had presided over the installation of the camp. We had been condemned to perish in our own dirt, to drown ourselves in mud, in our own excrements; the point was to abase us, to humiliate our human dignity, to drag us down to the level of the beasts, to fill us with horror and contempt for ourselves and our fellow-sufferers. That was the purpose, that was the idea of the camp! The Germans were perfectly aware of it; they knew that we prisoners had become incapable of looking at each other without disgust. There is no need to kill a prisoner in this camp in order to make him suffer; it is enough to give him a kick so that he falls in the mud. What rises up is not a human being, it is an absurd monster, plastered with filth'. (*Vingt Mois à Auschwitz*, pp. 61–62.) 'It was with complete awareness of what they were doing that the Germans defiled the best that there was among the peoples they conquered, defiled the most noble, forcing it to mingle with the most ghastly moral rottenness . . .' 'Human beings were inoculated quite consciously with the bacillus of depravity, so that they should be demoralized, slain morally and physically, as we destroy lice and noxious microbes; and, just like the lice which throve on our defenceless bodies, so the dregs of the camp, prostitutes, women thieves, offenders against the common law, penetrated into our social life: it was to these human dregs that the Germans had entrusted the task of watching over us and it was of them that they had made an *élite* under the name of "camp functionaries."'

One can see that, for the torturers, it was not a matter of immersing their victims in material conditions so abject that they were bound, in very many cases, to acquire from them the habits of animals; more subtly, it was a matter of degrading these victims morally by encouraging them to spy upon each other and by fomenting among the deported prisoners not only mutual resentment, but mutual suspicion; in short, of poisoning the wells of human relationship so that a prisoner who should have been, to another prisoner, a comrade and a brother, became instead an enemy, a demon, an incubus.

We are here in the presence of the *most monstrous collective crime in history*; only poisoned and poisonous imaginations could have conceived it in the first place; but what overwhelms one is the thought of the innumerable executive agents who were, after all, absolutely necessary if the insane idea was to become a working reality. We are only too well aware, for that matter, that these executive agents were very far from being all of German race or nationality; here, as elsewhere, a racial explanation of such horrors seems totally inadequate; we ought to be very glad of it, for I think it would be deplorable to turn against the Germans the wretched kind of argument which they themselves so pitifully and so stupidly misused. It hardly needs saying, I may note in passing, that ignoble acts of brutality and horseplay, such as the making compulsory of the wearing of the Star of David, and all the treatment that went with the wearing of that badge, which the Germans used against their Jewish victims before proceeding to their extermination, are other not less revealing examples of the techniques of degradation as I have defined them.

But here we are faced with an odd problem. Even if one forces oneself to see things from the point of view of the tormentors rather than of their victims, what rudiment of justification can one find for such methods? It might be alleged, no doubt, that it was in the interests of the torturers, for security reasons, to encourage every tendency in the camps that would keep their victims divided, that would prevent the growth of group courage and solidarity; for such solidarity could easily lead to acts of mutiny and rebellion.

And yet I feel very strongly that this utilitarian explanation, this explanation in terms of expediency, is inadequate. The wish to humiliate is a specific human disposition, which can quite certainly manifest itself without requiring any precise idea of an end to be gained; and it is very important for us at this point to try to get a notion of what this disposition is and what it implies. Theoretically, of course, we might be tempted to make the observation that the wish to humiliate and the wish to degrade could be two distinct dispositions, since a man can be degraded without becoming aware of his degradation. In actual practice, however, I think that this distinction soon reaches vanishing point; it is hardly possible that even the most radically degraded being should not sometimes be pierced by flashes of awareness and know the depth to which he has fallen. Let us notice, on the other hand, that the being whom one seeks to degrade is not necessarily the being in whom one has recognized a certain initial dignity. On the contrary, it may be just because one has denied the existence of this initial dignity that one has recourse to such methods. Indeed, the truth here is very subtle and perhaps almost impossible to grasp. How does a Streicher or a Himmler fundamentally estimate the Jew whom he is persecuting? Apparently he looks on this Jew as the rubbish, the waste, the leavings of the human race. But is not this irrational contempt the inverted expression of a feeling which in reality is much closer to envy? Is not ambivalence of feeling here more or less the rule?

The persecutor, at any rate, sets out to destroy in an another human being that being's awareness, whether illusory or not, of having a value. He must become for himself what those who judge him, or claim to judge him, say he is in reality; the person who is worth nothing must recognize his own nothingness, and it is not enough that he should do so intellectually; it is necessary also that he should *sense* his nothingness, as we sense an odour of decay that forces us to hold our noses. But why, in fact, is this necessary? First, once more, because this is the sole means of having this other human being wholly at one's mercy; a being who retains even the smallest awareness of his own value remains capable of reacting against us in a way which, if not dangerous, is at least vexing. On the other hand, in degrading his victim in this way, the persecutor strengthens in himself the sense of rightful superiority; he postulates that, from the beginning, his victim was already virtually the piece of waste product he has now for all practical purposes become, and it was therefore just to treat him with the utmost severity. In all this there is, from the logical point of view, a kind of hideous vicious circle which it is the duty of reflection to expose.

There is every reason to suppose also—and this is a point of capital importance from the point of view of the more general conclusions which I hope to draw later from these analyses—that the man who has perfected a technique of degradation, and is a past master in it, feels a delight and exaltation in applying it, comparable to the delight and exaltation of sacrilege. Here it would be necessary to proceed to a rather detailed analysis in order to bring out the sort of felt and living contradiction, without which sacrilege vanishes away. It does seem in fact, quite *a priori*, that sacrilege cannot exist except where there is a persistent awareness of the sacred; this awareness must persist just sufficiently for the infraction committed to retain its value *qua* infraction and, so to say, its savour; but it must not persist more strongly than that, for if it did a reverential fear might in the end prevent the sacrilegious person from carrying out his purpose. Might one say, however, that it is enough for the sacrilegious person to know that the sense of the sacred still persists among others; and that it is those others whom he sets out to shock and distress? I doubt, however, whether it is enough to speak of merely knowing that the sense of the sacred persists in others. I am led to believe that this sense must at least awaken in the sacrilegious person an echo, however distant and however soon silenced. An obvious comparison occurs to me here: we should think of these scenic railways, as some Luna Park or Magic City, with their regulated terrors, to which chattering adolescent girls throng; it is clear that if such young people felt no fear of the scenic railway, they would feel no pleasure either, but that if their terror reached a certain degree of intensity, their pleasure would vanish, too. In both cases, the terrible one and the innocent one, the existence of a felt contradiction dominates the experience and confers on it its specific quality.

Let us pass now to the point which I made earlier, that from the moment in which such techniques of degradation make their first appearance in the world, their use tends inevitably to become quite general.

The temptation to use these methods springs from the easiness of using them. And here we should no longer think of sacrilege, but of blackmail. When anybody possesses an almost infallible means of putting a person whom he holds at his mercy in a position in which the latter ceases to be an opponent worth reckoning with, to become instead a butt and a drudge, how is it possible that at the first opportunity, (or, if you like, on the smallest provocation) the man possessing such a power should not make use of it? It is obvious also that in the long run the victims of such persecution are likely to be contaminated by the example of their persecutors, and that if time brings in its revenges and puts these persecutors at their mercy the persecuted will be inevitably tempted to treat their persecutors as they themselves have been treated. Perhaps the action of God's grace is nowhere more clearly to be discerned than in the act by which a free being decides to break this hellish circuit of reprisals and counter-reprisals. But it must be said that in a world in which the techniques of degradation are becoming more and more generally operative this act of rupture is becoming, humanly speaking, more and more improbable.

So far we have considered the techniques of degradation in their most obviously shocking aspects; we shall have to push our analysis much farther if we are to recognize how firmly these techniques have taken root in our ordinary world to-day.

Let it be agreed, for instance, that in itself propaganda ought not to be classified among the techniques of degradation. We must recognize, nevertheless, that there is a close kinship between propaganda and the techniques of degradation; and to grasp the nature of that kinship, we must get a distinct notion of what propaganda is. Many of us still remember a time when, among political activities, propaganda had a relative and subordinate place. It was still propaganda *for* something, not propaganda in the absolute sense of the term. We had hardly then glimpsed the possibility of propaganda in that sense. Propaganda in those days meant merely the combined methods put into operation to recruit new adherents to some definite cause. To be sure, even in those days it was obvious that of its very nature propaganda was corruptible (not to say, corrupting); and this is even more true now that propaganda has become a method not of persuasion but of seduction. So long as I confine myself to bringing out the real reasons why I think the purposes to which I have devoted myself are useful or good, we cannot properly speak of seduction or corruption. The case is altered, when, by underhand means, I tend to put my emphasis specially on the adventitious benefits which someone else will gain by rallying to the same banner as myself. In all propaganda, of course, it is very difficult to draw a strict line between what is legitimate, and what is not; but it is obvious, for instance, that the bigger a part money plays in this sort of activity, the more the activity falls under suspicion.

But we get a much more dangerous situation when propaganda moves out of its original orbit; when it ceases to be exercised on behalf of a number of competing movements and parties within the State, and instead is taken over by the State itself; when the State, in short, begins to behave as if it were itself a movement or a party. Contemporary history shows us clearly enough that the scourge called 'the single party' paves the way for that other scourge, State propaganda. The single party is always the root from which modern dictatorships spring and from which they draw their strength. It is in this connection, I think, that the kinship between propaganda and the techniques of degradation can be seen most clearly.

There are some obvious objections, of course, to be dealt with here. Propaganda, it will be said, does not *aim* at degrading those on whom it has its effect. But this is true only up to a point. In spite of everything that can be said to the contrary, is not the real and deep purpose of propaganda after all that of reducing men to a condition in which they lose all capacity for individual reaction? In other words, whether the men in control of propaganda intend this or not, is it not of the very nature of propaganda to degrade those whose attitudes it seeks to shape? And is it possible to be unaware of the fact that propaganda presupposes, in these men in control, a fundamental contempt for the rest of the human race?. If we really attach any value at all to what a man is in himself, to his authentic nature, how can we assume the responsibility of passing him through the flattening-out machinery of propaganda?

What we ought to enquire into, however, is the nature of this contempt. There are, of course, fine shades of distinction that analysis ought to bring out: but is there any essential *difference* between the attitude of someone like Goebbels, for instance, and that of a chief of Communist propaganda? In both cases we are faced with a radical and cynical refusal to recognize the competence of individual judgment, an impatience with what appears, from this point of view, the intolerable presumptuousness of the individual. It is also broadly noteworthy that even the sense of truth cannot fail gradually and unconsciously to be destroyed in those who assume the task of manipulating opinion. It would require a very uncommon degree of simple-mindedness in a professional propagandist for him to remain very long convinced that *his* truth was *the whole truth*. Such simple-mindedness is only conceivable in a fanatic. But the fanatical temperament is generally *not* adapted for persuasiveness on a wide front; for seeking out these crooked and indirect paths by which an effective propagandist winds *into* the thought, and *under* the thoughts, of his auditor, in order to circumvent him. That is why tasks of this sort have so often been confided to renegades. To be sure, a renegade may himself become a fanatic, but it is with difficulty that he avoids retaining a certain imprint from his past, a certain ambivalence of attitude. And it is precisely in the renegade that we can find that fund of bad faith which, for the propagandist in general, is as necessary as a drawing account at the bank. In really effective propaganda, one has to know the state of mind of the opponent one is seeking to convince well enough to simulate, at least at the beginning, a certain sympathy with him; though one must take care, of course, to avoid basically identifying oneself with that state of mind. Effective propaganda, in short, is a matter of reconnoitring and exploiting as skilfully as possible the weaknesses of the enemy's position, while at the same time as little as possible giving the enemy the feeling that he *is* an enemy, that one is fighting him.

When the misdeeds of propaganda have been so clearly demonstrated as they have in the last few years, it seems time to question the premisses on which the case for propaganda rests. To question them, of course, at a moral rather than a practical level. Nobody is denying the practical possibility of manipulating opinion. On the contrary, we now know that opinion is the most malleable thing in the world. But ought we not to conclude, from that very fact, that opinion (in so far as I always find myself thinking of opinion as what *people* think, not as what *you* or *I* think; in so far as it seems to be something that floats from mind to mind like a murky cloud) is in itself something rather contemptible, which can never serve as a solid foundation for any social or political system? I cannot develop this train of thought here, and I shall confine myself to recalling the contrast I drew in a former work of mine between *faith* and *opinion*: though this contrast is being blurred to-day by an impure mode of thinking which tends to melt all categories together. Certainly, we cannot linger too long over the reflection that almost invariably to-day dictatorships start out as governments of opinion; a government of opinion nearly always, and as if by an inner destiny, ends by refusing to recognize the competence of individual opinion, in the way I have described; and, whether this refusal is based on a Hegelian or pseudo-Hegelian doctrine of the State, or a Nietzschean morality of Masters and Slaves, the practical consequences are the same in both cases.

What we now have to show is how technical progress in recent years has favoured this manipulation of opinion; and in particular we have to emphasize the prodigious part played in this process by radio. The Austrian writer, Joseph Roth, has thrown a clear light on the really satanic role which radio will be found to have played in contemporary history; but I doubt whether in general professional philosophers have so far concentrated their attention on this theme. How shall we be able to grasp the fact that radio is one of the palpable factors making for our present spiritual degradation? I should be tempted to ask whether man, at the level, which is nearly always a low level, of his personal ambition, is not usurping a prerogative which looks like a distorted analogue, a caricature, of divine omnipresence. A Hitler or a Mussolini, speaking into the microphone, could really seem invested with the divine privilege of being everywhere at once. In theory, of course, it is conceivable that this privilege of ubiquity, if it were at the service of a genuinely universal mode of thinking, could confer on that mode of thinking a wonderful and almost providential range of impact. But, in the first place, it is hardly conceivable that any leader of any State in our world to-day should be moved by the desire for a genuine universality; our most recent and most wretched experience shows us that the principles on which official propagandists put most emphasis are, in the vast majority of cases, a pitiful camouflage for their concealed purposes, which are marked by the most cynical imperialism.

In the second place, I fear that we must go further than this and ask ourselves whether there is not something in this mechanical method of diffusing thought which almost inevitably degrades whatever message men are seeking to diffuse. Moreover, I would say that it is not very difficult to find out the causes of this inevitable degradation, by the radio, of thought. Do they not lie in the fact that in the realm of radio man is attempting, without, however, this involving any real effort on his part, to transcend his human condition and the limitations it entails? It is, of course, not difficult to conceive that a saint might by some sudden miracle be invested, at least for a moment passing like a lightning flash, with this gift of ubiquity: that would only be a spatial transposition of his gift of charity, which in itself is independent of the *here* and the *now*. But how can we admit that such a miraculous gift can, without losing all its potency, be vested in the ordinary man? How can we allow that it is quite safe for any individual, whoever he is, to be granted the gift of being everywhere at once in return for the payment of an annual rent for radio time? Is there not a sort of usurpation here? And on the other hand do we not feel that something which is advantageous or good in itself, once it has been usurped, is liable in the long run to be put to evil uses?

I am not at all sure that all this could not be formulated in a much more general fashion: I am not sure that every kind of technical progress may not entail, for the individual who takes advantage of it *without having had any share in the effort at overcoming difficulties of which such a progress is the culmination*, the payment of a heavy price, of which a certain degradation at the spiritual level is the natural expression. Obviously, this does not mean that history can start moving backwards and that we ought to break all the machines: it means merely that, as Bergson with so much profundity observed, every kind of outward technical progress ought to be balanced in man by an effort at inner conquest, directed towards an ever greater self-mastery. Unhappily, what we still have to ask is whether for an individual who every day takes more and more advantage of the facilities which technical progress has put at his disposal, such an effort at self-mastery does not become more and more difficult. There is certainly every reason to suppose that it does. In our contemporary world it may be said that the more a man becomes dependent on the gadgets whose smooth functioning assures him a tolerable life at the material level, the more estranged he becomes from an awareness of his inner reality. I should be tempted to say that the centre of gravity of such a man and his balancing point tend to become external to himself: that he projects himself more and more into objects, into the various pieces of apparatus on which he depends for his existence. It would be no exaggeration to say that the more progress 'humanity' as an abstraction makes towards the mastery of nature, the more actual individual men tend to become slaves of this very conquest.

At the point we have now reached in this argument, broad horizons open out before us. We see superimposed on the relatively simple and particular notion of techniques aimed at degrading special groups of human beings, a notion of a much more general sort: we are about to ask ourselves whether, in certain conditions of which we must of course get a more exact idea, a technical progress which seems to be, of its nature, indifferent to moral values, but which is on the other hand the expression at the material level of a genuine intellectual conquest, is not itself in danger of becoming a method of human degradation; and indeed, when I have concluded this investigation of mine, it will be relevant to ask whether the fact that technical progress seems to be culminating to-day in the invention of more and more formidable instruments of destruction can be imputed to a mere chance concurrence of circumstances.

We ought to insist, however, that there would be no point in regarding either technical progress in general, or the progress of some particular technique, as having of its very nature a necessarily negative value for the spirit. It would be more precise to say that technical progress in the strict sense is a good thing, both good in itself, and good because it is the incarnation of a genuine power that lies in human reason: good even because it introduces into the apparent disorder of the outer world a principle of intelligibility. But the question we are faced with is this: what are the effects (not the necessary effects, but the probable effects) of technical progress on the man who takes advantage of it without having helped in any way to achieve it? Ought not the observations which I have already roughly outlined to direct us towards a deeper truth? Does not the invasion of our life by techniques to-day tend to substitute satisfaction at a material level for spiritual joy, dissatisfaction at a material level for spiritual disquiet? And do not the satisfied and the unsatisfied tend to come together in a common mediocrity? The fact is that to the average man to-day, whose inner life tends too often to be a rather dim affair in any case, technical progress seems the infallible method by which he can achieve a sort of generalized comfort, apart from which he finds it impossible to imagine happiness. I am bearing in mind also that this generalized comfort, with its appurtenances—standardized amusements, and so on—seems the only possible way to make life tolerable, when life is no longer considered as a divine gift, but rather as a 'dirty joke'. The existence of a widely diffused pessimism, at the level of the sneer and the oath rather than that of sighs and weeping, seems to me a fundamental given fact about contemporary humanity; and it seems to me that it is in the perspective of this widely diffused pessimism, a pessimism not so much thought out as retched forth, a sort of physical nausea at life, that we ought to consider such a serious and significant contemporary fact as the prevalence, for instance, of abortion.

Let us recall also the relevant fact that in an absurd or chaotic world technical achievements tend to seem more and more the chief, if not the only, mark of man's superiority to the animals. In this exaltation of techniques there might, of course, be a Promethean defiance, not without its own greatness and nobility. But, at the level of the consumer, such a defiance is degraded and perverted. Quite aside from the fact that technical progress, considered from the consumer's point of view, encourages a kind of laziness, it also fosters resentment and envy. These passions centre themselves on definite material objects, whose possession usually does not seem to be linked to any definite personal superiority, not even that superiority of refined taste which a lover of prints or china may show in building up his collection. Where a frigidaire or a radio-gramophone are in question, the very ideas of 'having' and 'possessing' acquire a sense which is at once provocative of bad feeling and spiritually hollow: 'He has the good luck to possess that gadget, and he didn't do anything for it; it does belong to him, of course, but it might just as well belong to me, and that would be fairer'. Between any sort of mechanical apparatus and its possessor there cannot be established that living, that almost latently spiritual relationship, that exists, for instance, between a small-holder and his piece of land: that exists there, because the very notion of the cultivation of the ground implies, also, the notion of an extraordinary exchange—a mutual, patient traffic between the land's fruitfulness and the peasant's care. But is it not rather the case that in the world where technique is triumphant this idea of 'exchange', though still persistent, has lost its old values: just because exchange in the true sense is not something mechanical? It implies, rather, an endless possibility of disappointment; for the owner of a vineyard, for instance, who has tended his vines with loving care throughout the year, may at the last moment see his grapes destroyed by a hailstorm. For him and for his like, there can be no guarantee of security. In the realm of mechanical technique, in theory at least, there is no danger of anything so distressing and shocking happening: in theory, I say, for in practice the effects of a bad harvest or an epidemic can impinge even on this protected area. But obviously the ideal at which technical progress is aiming is that of bringing into being a privileged realm: one on which these impingements of the unpredictable will no longer have any effect, and where guarantees of security will be utterly reliable.

Now, that the sort of thing I described a moment ago can happen to the peasant, is undoubtedly distressing and shocking; but, on the other hand, experience seems to show us that as soon as a preoccupation with security begins to dominate human life, the scope of human life itself tends to be diminished. Life, as it were, tends to shrink back on itself, to wither. One reason for this may be that the powers of initiative, among those who are not equipped to contribute effectively to scientific and technical progress, tend to exercise themselves as it were on the edge of things and even to degenerate into a mere power of subversion. That might be one of the more fundamental reasons why a period in history of highly developed techniques tends also to become a period of revolution. But we ought to ask ourselves also whether the will to subversion, in our world to-day, may not be linked to a precisely opposite disposition: to a sort of petty conservatism, narrowed down to the notion of conserving the individual's own skin; for the spirit that used to inspire a more generous type of popular conservatism, the spirit that inspired the workman to bring up a large family, is dying away, just where it used properly to exercise itself. It no longer makes men want to bring up and educate many children, it transfers itself to a level of mere talk where it is lost in words and smoke or, worse still, it expresses itself in physical violence and finally in the persecution of one human group by another one.

In such a train of events (the degradation of the conservative spirit in workmen from care for a family to political rant and finally to brutish violence), the degrading side of technical progress is displayed with the utmost clarity. The notion of life is degraded in the first place, and all the other degradations quite naturally follow. We might even ask whether the man who lives as a servant of technical progress does not come to regard life as a technique mainly: a very imperfect one, where slapdash work and botching are still the rule. Given such a point of view, how could such a man fail to claim for himself the right to interfere with the onflow of life, just as one dams a river? Before he decides to start a baby 'on the way', he will make careful calculations, just as if he were buying a motorcycle: he will try to estimate the annual expense as exactly as possible: foreseeing illnesses and doctors' bills in one case: wear and tear and garage expenses in the other. Fairly frequently, instead of a baby, he will decide, by way of economy, on a little dog. It costs less; and if the bills at the veterinary surgeon's grow too big, it can always be put painlessly out of the way. So far, to be sure, we have not envisaged this possibility in the case of sickly small children.

We could push this analysis much farther, and in quite other directions; at the level not of the individual and the family, but of the State and international life, what are the points of impact of a process which tends more and more towards the identification of science and power, at a level where the difference between science and technique in some regions of science at least, is becoming negligible? In a world in which the absolute hegemony of States or groups of States is being affirmed, how almost irresistible must be the temptation to confiscate new inventions, new patents, for the benefit of these monstrous powers! But competition between States for inventions must tend more and more to augment, the more intense it becomes, that collective application of technical power with which to-day the very notion of science tends to be confused. Just as, in the case of its effects on the individual, technical progress would be wholly a good thing if it were to remain at the services of a spiritual activity directed towards higher ends, so, at the international level, technical progress could be considered as a priceless gift if it were to be exercised on behalf of a unified mankind, or rather on behalf of mankind working together. But when this is not the case either for the individual or in relation to the great human collectivities, it becomes immediately obvious that technical progress is bound to be transformed from a blessing into a curse.

For that matter, there is not in this process, as some simple-minded people think, some sort of unintelligible calamity, like a cyclone or a cholera epidemic (which of course are neither of them strictly unintelligible either), but rather a price we have to pay for what, in a vocabulary unfamiliar to technical experts, we must simply call *sin*. One of the misfortunes of our time is that the use of this word is almost the private preserve of the clergy, whom hardly anybody listens to, and who, indeed, do not always know how to transcend the limits of a mode of speech, ancient and respectable, no doubt, but which seems sometimes quite unable to get to grips with real and visible evils. Once more, I ought to emphasize here that there would be no point in thinking of technical progress as being in itself the expression of sin. It is clear enough, indeed, that, at our present period in history, as soon as the techniques on which civilized life rests yield before hostile pressures, a return to barbarous conditions sets in with disconcerting rapidity. On the other hand, it is also clear that technical progress is increasingly tempting man to claim for his achievements at this level an intrinsic value that cannot really belong to them. Quite simply, we can say that there is a danger of technical progress making men into idolaters.

If men are generally unaware of this danger, it is because they are deceived by their own childish notion of idolatry. Idolatry is something that savages do! It consists of adoring queer little fetishes! How could the mechanic or the emancipated 'little man', who pride themselves in believing nothing, be idolaters? Have they not freed themselves from all superstitions? But their delusion consists precisely in failing to recognize that superstition can work itself into the very substance of the mind: to use an unpleasant image, one might say that superstition becomes encysted in the modern consciousness, instead of breaking out in a warning rash on the surface. The man who 'believes in nothing' does not really exist, any more than the man who clings to nothing, who holds to nothing: and to believe in something and to cling or hold to it are at bottom very much the same mental act. People forget this, because they tend to lump 'believing in' something together with 'forming' or 'holding' an 'opinion' about it. That, however, is a blunder: for it does very often happen that our 'opinions', under analysis, can be seen to be not mental acts but mere mental habits. In practice, they reduce themselves to things which we habitually say in a certain context, without asking ourselves what our words mean or how they would be applied in the actual world: in fact, we should often feel 'caught out', if someone asked us to put our opinions into practice. On the other hand, we really only 'believe in' something which we do in practice cling to or hold to: now, to cling or hold to something is to have some sort of living link with it; the man who believes in nothing, like the man who clings to nothing, can have no such links. But such a man is notional or even chimerical. He cannot actually exist. Existence without living links is not concretely conceivable. It is not among real possibilities.

What we have still to ask ourselves, however, is what becomes of these living links, which the very notion of existence presupposes, in the case in which not only belief in the full sense, belief in God, but belief in others and even perhaps belief in life have disappeared. What becomes then of the moral tissue of human behaviour? I would ask the reader to pause thoughtfully over this word 'tissue'; I have long thought that in the long run it is histology which provides the most apt and concrete metaphors for our thinking about, and our descriptions of, moral life. What is the 'tissue' of a man who no longer (at least obviously) 'believes in' anything—what holds him together? On what can the attention of such a man be directed? I would say quite bluntly and flatly: on himself. What exactly do we mean here, however, by 'himself'? The self on which his attention is directed must consist in the first place of sensations, and perhaps also of that transposition of visceral conditions into psychological states which culminates in self-satisfaction or dissatisfaction with oneself. But, at this level, what exactly is the nature of dissatisfaction with oneself? It is essentially a kind of dyspepsia. I do not know a more revealing popular expression, in this connection, than the phrase about 'not being able to stomach' something which somebody has said or done to me. It is a curious and significant fact, also, that, in French, this verb can be used only in a negative sense. (In English, of course, people *can* say, 'I can just stomach' so-and-so or such-and-such.) We never, in French, say, 'I *can* stomach' something or other. As for the things I cannot stomach, they are generally of the following sort: the fact that someone I know has received a promotion or a decoration or inherited a small sum of money: or the way in which somebody spoke to me about my wife, my servant, or my colleague at the office. In short, what I cannot stomach is somebody else just in so far as he *is* somebody else, a clog on or an impediment to my own life. To be fair, however, we should notice that this failure to 'stomach' one's neighbour need not necessarily take the form of envy: it may be that I am unable to stomach the wretched poverty of the man next door, a poverty which prevents me from enjoying my own crumb of comfort in peace and quiet.

To sum up our drift so far and to prepare the way for the general conclusions that are going to be forced on us, let us make the following statement: a civilization in which technical progress is tending to emancipate itself more and more from speculative knowledge, and finally to question the traditional rights of speculative knowledge, a civilization which, one may say, finally denies the place of contemplation and shuts out the very possibility of contemplation, such a civilization, I say, sets us inevitably on the road towards a philosophy which is not so much a *love of wisdom* as a *hatred of wisdom*: we ought rather to call it a misosophy. For, in the last analysis, we may ask ourselves how it is possible on such foundations to erect anything at all resembling what has traditionally been understood by the word 'wisdom'. It seems to me, for instance, almost certain that the notion of authentic wisdom implies references to a level of reality which is wholly left out of the calculations of a man like Sartre when he makes his contrast between 'being-in-itself' (corresponding to what has been traditionally called 'matter') and 'being-for-itself', corresponding not so much to what has traditionally been called 'mind' as to a kind of interior collapse. Let us remember, in addition, that Sartre at all times and in all situations is very ready to attack what he calls 'serious-mindedness'. But this serious-mindedness is something which the very notion of wisdom, if wisdom is not to be degraded into a sort of sneering buffoonery, does most definitely imply. This is true even of pessimistic thinkers of the great tradition; for them, there is at least *something* which must be taken seriously, and that is the verdict which the wise man or the holy man finds himself forced to pass on a world of illusion and madness; but surely this verdict itself requires the wise man or the saint to transcend the world of illusion and madness—and transcendence, in this sense, is something for the possibility of which Sartre and his friends seem to me to make no allowances.

In this chapter, then, we have started by considering techniques of degradation at their most deliberate and systematic, the techniques which aim at degrading some given category of men—of degrading them *in their own eyes*. It is easy to see that it is only possible to make use of such techniques in a world in which universal values are being systematically trampled underfoot; and by 'universal values' here, I do not wish to emphasize particularly notions like 'goodness as such', 'truth as such'—that is a type of Platonism of which I am hardly an adherent. It is not a matter merely of the *idea* of the good or the true being trampled on, but of these values being trampled on in their living scope and actual relations: being trampled on in so far as they confer on human existence its proper dignity—in so far as they confer that on *every* human existence. In this connection, I should notice in passing, it is quite impossible to acquit Nietzsche of a certain at least indirect responsibility for the horrors of which we have been, and still are, the witnesses. We ought not, of course, to be deceived by a philosopher's special vocabulary; and when Nietzsche talked about getting 'beyond good and evil', we should recognize that he wanted to lay the foundations for a higher kind of good. It is none the less true—and either Nietzsche failed to perceive this, or he was very wrong in thinking himself not bound to take it into consideration—that, at the level of experience, Nietzsche's 'beyond' becomes a 'beneath'; his way up is, in practice, a way down: not a transcendence of ordinary moral categories but, to use a word coined by Jean Wahl, a transdescendence from them.

Whatever we may think in the long run of Nietzsche's contrast between the morality of slaves and that of masters, even admitting that there is a context in which it might make good sense, it is quite obvious that, given a crude historical application, that antithesis could only itself become degraded and give rise to worse aberrations than itself. As soon as one cynically postulates that, whether for reasons of race or class, a certain category of human beings can have no share in certain human values—as soon as one has done that, so soon one finds, by a kind of reactive shock, that it is the values one imagines oneself to be defending that one is making unreal. In another vocabulary, but in one with many affinities to the previous one, we might say that these abominable techniques of degradation can be put into operation only if one refuses to regard man as being made in the image of God; or one might even say quite simply, when one refuses to regard man as a created being. All this is too obvious to be worth insisting on. On the other hand, the converse of the above proposition seems to me extremely significant and, at the moment of history at which we have now arrived, deserving of deep consideration: *so soon as man denies to himself that he is a created being*, a double peril faces him: on the one hand he will be led—and this is exactly what we see in Sartre's type of existentialism—to claim for himself a kind of *self-dependence* which caricatures that of the Deity. He will be led, that is, to consider himself as a being who makes himself and *is* only what he makes of himself; for if there is nobody who can destroy his self-sufficiency, similarly there is no gift which can be made to that sufficiency; a being conceived as Sartre conceives man is utterly incapable of receiving anything. But from another point of view, and yet in a closely connected way, the man who conceives himself as Sartre conceives man will be led to think of himself as a sort of waste product of a universe which is, for that matter, an inconceivable universe—so that we see such a man, at the same time and for the same set of reasons, exalting and abasing himself beyond all just measure. For that matter, we ought to add that, strange as it may seem, this self-abasement will have an exhilarating effect; it will enable our Sartrian man to procure a kind of joy for himself, just as having themselves whipped, for some people, is a condition of erotic pleasure . . . I have spoken, however, of this Sartrian self-exaltation and self-abasement as being *beyond all just measure:* it may be asked, where are we to get our measure from: to what other levels of being can man, after all, be properly related or compared? Will it be said that we must come back, quite simply, to the formula of the Greek sophist: 'man is the measure of all things'. That, in fact, is a possibility. But the formula itself is a strangely ambiguous one, for it throws no light at all on just how man comes to understand himself and judge himself. But we can also perhaps say with considerable plausibility that the moral relativism implied in the formula, 'Man is the measure of all things', puts us on a path that will in the long run lead us to a degraded kind of humanism: a humanism that is parasitic on nature, as moss is parasitic on a tree.

Our first theme, in this chapter, then, was modern techniques of degradation at their most systematic and deliberate; we were led to consider, thereafter, such a technique as propaganda, which can only in fact degrade those on whom it is exercised, and which presupposes, in those who exercise it, an utter contempt for those on whom it is exercised. In a word, every kind of propaganda implies a claim to have the right to manipulate other men's consciences. Following on the heels of the abject ferocity of the concentration camps, what we here witness is the spirit of imposture. We should notice, also, the inevitable connection between these two aspects of a single scourge. For how would it be possible not to take the most severe, the most inhuman steps against those who refuse to let themselves be indoctrinated and who become, consequently, opponents who must be put down by any means available? Propaganda is a cynical refusal to recognize that ordering of man's awareness in subordination to truth which it is the imperishable glory of the great rationalist philosophers, whatever may have been their metaphysical errors, to set in the clearest light. But what is truth? That is the question that may be asked with insulting irony by the man who, as a propagandist, is a past master in the art of shaping opinion according to his fancy. It is obvious that this Machiavellian attitude, in all its forms, implies a flat refusal to recognize the claims of Socrates and of all his philosophical posterity—the eternal claim to seek truth, and nothing but truth. And in this fact, or so it seems to me, we can find a grave and solemn warning to all those who, in the name of class prejudice or race prejudice, have repudiated the very notion of universality: a warning even, at a much deeper level of significance, to those who claim to substitute (and at some periods in my life this has perhaps been my own case) for the traditional philosophical categories that have been organized round the notion of truth, new tragic categories, like those of self-commitment, belief as a wager, life as the taking of a risk. Obviously, the intrinsic value of these existential notions is not something that can be denied: but only on condition that they are kept in their place, in the place that can be properly assigned to them, that is to say in subordination to grander structures which ought not, themselves, to be called into question. For there will always be a danger that what, for exceptional individualities, presents itself as a tragic philosophy, with its own undeniable grandeur, may become at the mass level a mere pragmatism for the use of middlemen and adventurers.

After dealing with these points, I was led, in this chapter, into raising an extremely general problem, a problem bearing on the spiritual and intellectual crimes attributable to what one might call a sort of *pantechnicism*, or possibly a general emancipation of techniques. Once again, this is not a matter of attributing criminality to techniques considered in themselves. For where techniques fulfil their proper functions, they are subordinated to something higher; there is no such thing, at the proper level of technical function, as a technique *in se*. The idea of the nature of something *in itself* is not relevant when we are talking of something, such as a technical process, which exists for purposes *outside itself*. But the case is radically altered when technical knowledge begins to claim a sort of primacy in relation to modes of thinking, like my own, that concentrate on being rather than doing. It should be clear to readers who have followed my work for some time that these remarks are a development of those I made, more than ten years ago, about the notion of *function*, in so far as this contrasts with that of an actual grip on being, of any sort. In the claims of technical knowledge to primacy and in the way in which a concentration on mere technical functioning is opposed to an actual grasp of reality we have, no doubt, two manifestations of the same evil, the same flinching of the human spirit. But what ought to strike us more than anything else about what I have called the emancipation of techniques is the fact that what starts off as a collection of means put together to serve an end outside itself tends, after all, in the long run to be valued and cultivated for its own sake; and in consequence to become the centre, the focus, of an obsessive cult. It is in this way that the abuse of technical knowledge and technical processes is in danger, as I have already indicated in passing, of giving rise to an actual idolatry: an idolatry which, to be sure, is not recognized as such, its very nature excluding any such recognition.

The purpose of such evidence on this topic as I have endeavoured to assemble here is to help us to get our bearings in an investigation into the conditions which are undoubtedly likely to prevail in a world more and more completely given over to technical processes. Obviously, this world will require a growingly extended human agreement about its desirability; it is clear enough that no technical process can flourish independently of other technical processes. And at a first glance, this observation might seem of a sort to encourage us in a kind of optimism about the progress of human solidarity. But, to be honest, it does not seem to me that more prolonged reflection will be able to justify such optimism. What we have to fear, in fact, is that it is not among *men* that this solidarity is fated to be established, but rather among *submen*. It will be established, I mean, among beings who tend more and more to be reduced to their own strict function in a mechanized society, though with a margin of leisure reserved for amusements from which the imagination will be more and more completely banished. With this in mind, we might be tempted to ask what is, I agree, a rather paradoxical question. Observers have noted that in many countries to-day the majority of those whose tasks are purely functional seem to be suffering from a severe attack of laziness, or apathy. Is it not possible that this laziness may correspond to an obscure but necessary impulse of self-defence—of self-defence against a mortal danger to which most factory hands, for instance, exposed themselves quite light-heartedly when they first became cogs in the wheel?

I am far from asserting that such tasks involve, for every individual engaged in them, a *necessary* degradation. But what we can say is that it becomes less and less probable, in a world given over to techniques, that the individual will be able to free himself from a set of constraints, of which many appear, at first, less as constraints than as seductions; that is strictly the case, for instance, not only in relation to propaganda, but in relation to all its ancillary operations at the level of publicity or pusedo-art. And that is not the whole story; for in such a world the proper domain of truth is more and more ignored and abandoned, and so quite naturally, as we have seen, imposture tends to proliferate like a fungus, with the help of these technical methods which every quack, to-day, can use to sell his elixirs to the gullible. But there are other points we ought to emphasize here. I am thinking especially of the extraordinary degradation in our time of discussion, the very bases of discussion; a degradation to which each succeeding day, in France, bears melancholy witness. To dispose of your opponent, or to put him down for the count, it is enough, in France to-day, to stick an obnoxious label on him and then to fling in his face, as one might a bottle of acid, some gross accusation to which it is impossible for him to reply; your opponent being completely confounded by such tactics, it will be said that he admits your case and capitulates. Thus, in certain circles in France to-day, it would be impossible to utter a balanced judgment on certain historical figures of our time and the intentions they may have started out with, without being automatically classed among those who approve of the methods of Buchenwald and Auschwitz. That, however, is just one example, among many possible other ones, of the sort of thing I am talking of. What is glaringly obvious is that this sense of the fine shades of truth, so inseparable from the sense of truth itself, is being literally stifled to-day by partisan passions. To be sure, a rather long analysis would be necessary if we were to attempt to show in detail how inevitable it is, in such a world as I have described, that these passions should spawn and multiply: but it cannot escape anyone that there does exist between partisan passions and propaganda a reciprocal soliditary, the reciprocal solidarity almost of premisses and conclusions in a viciously circular argument. The propaganda incites the passions, the passions in their turn justify the excesses of the propaganda.

At all events, any man who puts himself under the influence of that spirit of imposture, which is the spirit of propaganda, will gradually be contaminated to the point at which, even in his own proper sphere of activity, he is ready to participate in deception. What one can say, no doubt, is that novices in imposture are generally not in a state to become aware of how far they are deliberately deceiving themselves and others, but this very fact makes their situation almost desperate: how, in fact, can we hope to cure them of a malady whose early symptoms they are incapable of discovering?

At this point we ought to make a strict synthesis of all our observations so far, and we ought to show, in particular, how the spirit of imposture almost invariably thrives best in a world given over to resentment. Obviously, between the growth in men of a mood of resentment and that general emancipation of techniques that we have been describing, it is not possible, at a first glance, to grasp any direct connection. But what ought to be understood is that technical man (if I may call him so), having in the deepest sense lost his awareness of himself—having lost, above all, that is, his awareness of these transcendental laws which allow him to guide his behaviour and direct his intentions—is becoming more and more completely disarmed in the face of the powers of destruction unleashed around him and in the face, also, of the spirit of complicity which these powers encounter in the depths of his own nature.

For in the long run all that is not done through Love and for Love must invariably end by being done against Love. The human being who denies his nature as a created being ends up by claiming for himself attributes which are a sort of caricature of those that belong to the Uncreated. But how should this pretended or parodic human autarchy that modern man usurps for himself not degenerate into a resentment turned back on the very self for which such absurd claims are made? And that resentment flows out into the techniques of degradation. There is a road that could be marked out by a succession of signposts leading from the abortionists to the death camps where torturers rage and sate themselves on a population of defenceless victims.

CHAPTER IV

TECHNICAL PROGRESS AND SIN

ONE extremely general fact appears to me to dominate the contemporary situation. Men have entered into what we are forced to call the eschatological age. I do not necessarily mean by this that what we call, in what must in any case be an equivocal phrase, 'the end of the world' is near to us in time; it would seem to me rash and even childish to attempt to prophesy. But what matters is that the human race as a species must appear to us to-day as endowed with the power, if it wants to, of putting an end to its own earthly existence. This is not a matter only of a vague, distant possibility, evoked by some cranky astronomer from the depths of his observatory—it is a matter of a near, of an immediate possibility, a possibility whose basis lies in man himself, not in the sudden irruption of some heavenly body, bringing with it cosmic catastrophe.

This very general fact, then, contains implications of every kind on which the philosopher cannot concentrate with too much attention. But it is necessary as a preliminary to grasp the fact in all its amplitude. The atom bomb, for instance, is to all appearances only one particular illustration and, as it were, symbolic summary of a given state of affairs which has much more to do than the atom bomb has with the very essence of our condition.

Some time ago I read, in a daily paper, this: 'The echoes of Bikini had hardly died away when Dr Gerald West, broadcasting from Schenectady, declared that the special division of the American services dealing with chemical warfare had perfected a new toxic substance of extraordinary power. Though in appearance this substance seems to consist of perfectly harmless crystals, one ounce of it would be enough to cause the deaths of the whole human population of the United States and Canada'. Now, whether Dr West's information was true to the actual facts or not—and I admit that in the sequel a partial denial of his story was issued—what is peculiarly important and significant is that his story could be broadcast: one might well ask whether the very fact that such a broadcast can be issued does not in some sense condemn the civilization in which it takes place. For, in fact, what does this announcement of Dr West's tell us but that a technique has been discovered in comparison to which the exploits of the most famous criminals in history amount to mere child's play? On the other, this broadcast had a *meaning*, it was not put over without a fairly obvious purpose; and that purpose was surely not merely, as in the case of films and plays of the 'horror' type, to allow the public the pleasure of a voluptuous shiver. It is all too clear that the broadcast had some sort of definite relation with those toxological investigations of which it aimed at announcing the results. Its purpose, in a word, was intimidation. We are in the presence here of blackmail on a world scale.

It may be said that such blackmail is obviously a reaction to blackmail from another quarter: blackmail more veiled possibly, but just as threatening. But, if one replies to blackmail with blackmail, one is rendering oneself in some sense the accomplice of whoever started blackmailing first. One puts oneself, at least, in a position from which one cannot utter a valid condemnation of this other 'who started it'; and one descends into an infernal circle from which, if we consider the merely human possibilities of the situation, if we remain below the level of miracle, there is no way out. For it is all too obvious that this attempt to intimidate one's opponent, this putting him on his guard, can only act as an incitement. The one 'who started it' must now see himself as in a state of legitimate defence, and he must draw a certain inner strength from that new view of himself: this is exactly the fashion in which a firm retort to the opponent seems to become a kind of complicity in his scheme. For, in other countries, there can be no lack of well qualified and state-supported chemists in whom Dr West's warning must merely stimulate their natural self-esteem and their talents for discovery. So, and this must be said as bluntly as possible, in this little anecdote we see crime and stupidity walking hand in hand. We may, of course, attempt to persuade ourselves that the very growing frightfulness and inhumanity of these weapons, and the possibilities of doing evil that they represent, will, so long as two parties are engaged in this kind of arms race, tend to hold these two parties reciprocally in check. But the idea of a durable peace founded on mutual blackmail and intimidation comes up against psychological impossibilities on which contemporary history, for that matter, has thrown a sufficiently clear light.

I have called this chapter 'Technical Progress and Sin': and the general direction of the thoughts that follow is, I imagine, already sufficiently apparent. One must admit, however, that the use of the term 'sin', at a level of discussion which is that of philosophy and not of theology, may arouse certain objections. Is not sin in its very essence the rebellion of the creature against his Creator, and can this word retain any meaning for the unbeliever whose own position is precisely that God the Creator does not exist? Such an objection seems to have an incontestable formal validity. But if we go a little deeper, we shall have, it seems to me, to recognize that unbelievers themselves, faced with the abuses, with the systematic horrors, which we have seen become more and more widespread in the last thirty years, have acquired a growing awareness of the note of sin that is the mark of such monstrosities—and this even though we have witnessed during the same period a certain regression of public morality. In this fact there is a paradox to which it may be useful to draw attention. There is nobody, a few monstrous exceptions apart, who does not become indignant, or who dares to confess indifference, when confronted with the fact of the innumerable crimes of which the wholly innocent were victims during the last war. I am thinking particularly of children who died in concentration camps, but also of those who perished in bombing raids. To me, it seems very difficult to find any sort of argument that can even attempt to excuse this general crime against human life. A partisan propaganda has, of course, at its disposal certain resources: it will denounce such crimes when committed by the enemy, conceal them or brazenly deny them when committed 'by our own side'. Naturally, we must deprive ourselves of such resources. Resolutely and deliberately, we must draw back from such propaganda; for, as I shall no doubt have occasion enough to repeat, from whatever source it emanates, it poisons everything it touches. Yet though an indefinitely large number of individuals have their thinking shaped by this tentacular propaganda, still a good many of these individuals—I should be tempted even to say, the vast majority of them—preserve a healthy reaction when they are brought directly face to face with the horrors which previously they had only heard about. And in the end that is what matters; for in the long run the great heaps of lies crumble, and reality appears as it is.

This almost universal emotion in the face of horror—an emotion, it may be admitted, that has so far had no appreciable effect in preventing horrors from occurring—is the coming to the surface of a deep sense of piety towards life; and that at an epoch where thought at the more conscious and rationalizing level is being led more and more into denying that life has any 'sacred' character; and it is in connection with this spontaneous piety, but as outraging it (and more often than not quite independently of any positive religious attachment, of any link with historical revelation), that these acts, which we have been the witnesses or victims of, seem to us to bear the undeniable mark of sin.

Whatever attempts there may have been in the past to justify war, or at least to recognize a certain spiritual value in war, we ought to proclaim as loudly as possible that war with the face it wears to-day is sin itself. But at the same time we cannot fail to recognize that war is becoming more and more an affair of technicians: it presents to-day the double aspect of destroying whole populations without distinction of age or sex, and of tending more and more to be conducted by a small number of individuals, powerfully equipped, who direct operations from the safe depths of their laboratories. The fate of war and that of technical advancement, in our time, whether or not this conjunction is a merely accidental one, seem to be inextricably linked; and it can be asserted even that, at least in our present phase of history, everything that gives a new impetus to technical research at the same time renders war more radically destructive, and bends it more and more inexorably to what, at the breaking point, would be quite simply the suicide of the human race.

In a strange way, this connection between technical progress and sin becomes clearer if we remember on the one hand that to-day only the State is rich enough to finance the gigantic laboratories in which the new physics is being applied and developed; and on the other hand that, in a world given over like our own to rival imperialisms, the State itself, that 'Great Leviathan', to use the phrase of Hobbes, is inevitably led to demand that such researches should be directed towards everything that can increase the power of the State in its coming conflict with its rivals. It is in relation to these facts that we are forced to assert that the growing state-control of scientific and technical research is one of the worst calamities of our time.

When we reflect on it, however, this tragic situation of ours is very far from appearing a *natural* situation. We cannot say that the realm of the technical is evil in itself or that progress at the technical level ought, as such, to be condemned. Even to pretend that this were so would be to relapse into childishness. We can immediately see, even though it is perhaps impossible to discover the logical basis for this opinion, that it would be absurd to hope to solve the present crisis by closing down the factories and the laboratories for good and all. There is every reason to suppose, on the contrary, that such a step would be the starting point of an almost unimaginable regression for the human race.

The truth is that if we want to state the problem of the relationship between technical progress and sin in acceptable terms we must go back to first principles. In the last analysis, what *is* a technique? It is a group of procedures, methodically elaborated, and consequently capable of being taught and reproduced, and when these procedures are put into operation they assure the achievement of some definite concrete purpose.

As I have just been saying, the realm of the technical, as thus defined, is not to be considered as evil in itself; if we think of it in itself, as I have already said, a technique is rather something good or the expression of something good, since it amounts to nothing more than a specific instance of our general application of our gift of reason to reality. To condemn technical progress is, therefore, to utter words empty of meaning. But from the point of view of truth, what we must do is not to cling to our abstract definition but rather to ask ourselves about the concrete relationship that tends to grow up between technical processes on the one hand and human beings on the other; and here things become more complicated.

In so far as a technique is something that we can acquire, it may be compared to a possession—like habit, which is at bottom itself already a technique. And we can at once see that if a man can become the slave of his habits, it is equally probable that he can become the prisoner of his techniques. But we have to go deeper. The truth is that a technique, for the man whose task it is *to invent it*, does not present itself simply as a means; for a time at least, it becomes an end in itself, since it has to be discovered, to be brought into being; and it is easy to understand how a mind absorbed in this task of discovery can be drawn away from any thought of the real purpose to which, in principle, this technique ought to be subordinate. To take a simple example, it is clear enough that a technician to whom, for one reason or another, travelling is impossible or forbidden, might nevertheless devote himself to the improvement of design in motor-cars. I should be tempted to say that all technical progress implies a certain moral and intellectual outlay (of attention, ingenuity, perseverance, and so on) which betrays itself by a feeling of power or of pride; in which fact, of course, there is nothing that is not usual and allowable. Such feelings are the natural accompaniment of inventive activity. But they become unnatural, as we have already seen, they lose their just pretext and their authenticity, in the case of the man who benefits from an invention without having made any contribution towards discovering and perfecting it. We can understand this if we think of the state of mind of certain motorists who acquire a kind of passion for their car, spend their time swapping one car for another, and thus become less and less capable of considering the car as what it is, a means for getting about. The lack of curiosity of the passionate motorist is a fact of common experience. But this remark has a much more general application, and is true for instance also of radio enthusiasts. What we are noticing here is the passage from the realm of the technical, properly so called, to that of a kind of idolatry of which technical products become the object or at least the occasion. And if we follow out this line of reflection, we can see that even this kind of idolatry can degenerate into something worse; it can become *autolatry*, worship of oneself, and often does so in those circles where people can get excited only about records, especially speed records. Certainly, there is a great deal here that we ought to go into more deeply; we could ask ourselves how it is that speed has come to be regarded as an end rather than a means, how it has come to be sought out for its own sake—and we ought to contrast such a state of mind with that of the traveller of the old days, and particularly of the pilgrim, for whom the very slowness of progress was linked to a feeling of veneration. The transformation that has taken place in these matters seems to have even metaphysical significance. In a very general way, we might say that the exaltation of speed records goes hand in hand with a weakening, an attenuation, of the sense of the sacred.

But let us consider another much more general and much more important aspect of the same phenomenon. One might say that the notion of technical progress, at least in our own day, implies above all the notion of progress in communications. The perfecting of means of transport has been to all appearances the condition (while at the same time, of course, one of the effects) of the industrialization which has been proceeding with an accelerating rhythm during the past century. But what we must concentrate our powers of reflection on is just this very notion of communication, taken in a quite external sense. That the world should cease to be divided into many little compartments, that the country folk, in particular, should cease to live, in their own little closed regions, an entirely local life, a life with no relation to that of other neighbouring groups, all that seems to me an infinitely happy transformation, and one which by itself would serve to justify the belief in progress. But we must be careful here. Naturally, it is true to say that this general development of communications *can* or *could*—or ought to be able to—produce excellent results: that, for instance, where some new good thing has been discovered, the development of communications guarantees a widespread use of this good thing that would not have been imaginable a century ago. Let us think, for instance, of medicines (serums or penicillin) taken by aeroplane to sick people who, without such outside help, would undoubtedly have died. But this good possibility is only one possibility among many; we ought to ask ourselves whether there are not also evil possibilities whose very principle is to be found just in this perfecting of communication, in a quite external sense, of which we have been talking.

Do we not find, both on the world scale and at the level of national existence, that the development of communications entails a growing uniformity imposed upon our customs and habits? In other words, this perfecting of communications is achieved everywhere at the expense of an individuality which is tending to-day more and more to vanish away: and we are thinking here of beliefs, customs, traditions, as well as of local costumes, local craftsmanship, and so on. If we were taking a quite superficial view of human psychology and history, we might be tempted to say that this elimination of the picturesque is the unavoidable price that we pay for a greater good; for this reduction of habits to a general uniformity might, of course, be the beginning of a genuine unification of mankind. But our contemporary experience allows us to say quite definitely that there is nothing in this argument and that the imposing of uniformity, far from setting men on the path towards a kind of concrete assimilation of the universal, seems on the contrary to develop in them narrowly particular loyalties of a more and more aggressive sort, and to set competing groups against each other.

This might seem quite paradoxical, but reflection clears up the difficulty. Is it not obvious that technical and industrial progress have combined to create for men a kind of lowest common denominator of well-being which becomes an inspirer of covetousness and everywhere gives rise to envy? At the bottom, this lowest common denominator is merely wealth, one might say it is merely cash; but in saying that one should add that, by a very disturbing dialectical process, just as money becomes the lowest common denominator of well-being, so money itself tends to lose all substantial or even apparent reality, to become, in short, a fiction. After all, envy is only possible on the basis of what might be called a common drawing-account; it is less conceivable as existing between individuals and between peoples who have each their own traditions and their own separate genius, of which they are rightly proud. To be sure, this originality of each local and national tradition in respect to every other one has been very far, throughout history, from excluding quarrels and wars; up to a certain point, it has even encouraged them. But these quarrels, these wars, however bloody they may have been, did retain a human character; they did not exclude mutual respect, they made real reconciliations possible. There is nothing in them which at all resembles these attempts at collective extermination of which I spoke at the beginning of this chapter. But, besides all this, it would be of the greatest interest to discover by what odd mechanism ideological conflicts, to-day, conflicts sometimes quite without deep significance, have been able to superimpose themselves on elementary—and alimentary—antagonisms whose sole basis can finally be seen as envy.

It can, of course, always be claimed that this common drawing fund for envy, this lowest common denominator, however regrettable its immediate consequences may be, was none the less necessary, and that in the long run the current growth of uniformity will allow men to form a really organic and harmonious single body. It is difficult to make any judgment on such prophecies. But what must be recognized, it seems to me, speaking in all good faith, is that, if we consider things in a purely rational fashion, we can find no serious reason for expecting an *automatically* favourable outcome to the crisis which mankind is going through to-day. One cannot help observing that those ideological conflicts, which I have just been alluding to, tend to-day, so to say, to *make themselves at home* even in small country villages where, in the past, a friendly good-will prevailed and where to-day we can see the reign of mutual fear and suspicion. It is, of course, still possible to say that this is a purely transitional state of affairs; but the truth is that nobody sees how the state of affairs can be bettered in a way that would suit the aspirations of those who love peace and who also love what Victor Hugo called 'concord among citizens'. In reality, unless we have recourse to an act of faith, perfectly legitimate in itself and from the reilgious point of view even requisite, but quite foreign to the spirit of the man of mere technique, we should have to say that the malady from which mankind to-day appears to be suffering is perhaps mortal, and that there is nothing, at the purely human level, which insures our race against that risk of collective suicide of which I spoke at the beginning of this chapter.

But the mere mention of such an act of faith forces us to look at things from a higher level, and to define more precisely the world in which techniques are taking root. I must now venture into a more difficult and more strictly philosopihcal realm, and appeal to a set of ideas which it has been my task to elucidate over a period of about thirty years.

In the first place, it is obvious that there is no technical process which is not either actually or potentially at the service of some human desire or fear. We can say that all techniques exist in relation to man, in so far as man is moved by desire or fear. But the world of desire and fear is that of the problematic. I do not merely mean that the realization of any given desire or fear of mine has always a hypothetical character. The word 'problem' should be understood here with its Greek root in mind: *problema*. There is a problem when anything is placed *in front of me*, blocking my way; and on the other hand this self of mine, which finds itself faced by the problem, whose activity comes into play to solve the problem, remains above or below, however one likes to put it, remains beyond, in any case, those given elements which it has to deal with and handle if the desired solution of the problem is going to be found. Will it be said that this calculating and investigating self of mine gives rise to other problems, that there is, in other words, a possibility and even an obligatory possibility of this self placing itself, in the manner of an obstacle, in front of itself? But this is merely to push the difficulty one stage back! At all events, it will remain necessary to hold that the subject cannot pose or solve objective problems except on condition of itself remaining in a non-problematical sphere. Are we here verging on the idea, so familiar in Kantian and post-Kantian philosophy, of a transcendental ego or a pure subject? I do not really think so. Kant's transcendental ego is something chimerical or, at best, a convenient fiction; for when I think of this transcendental ego, and however careful I am to describe it as a pure subject, I am nevertheless, *by* thinking of it, treating it as an object: but as an object to which I paradoxically deny all the determinate characteristics by which any real object is defined. And it is at this point, therefore, that I am led to introduce or to reinstate into our vocabulary the notion of mystery, in opposition to the notion of problem.

What, then, is mystery? In contrast to the world of the problematic which, I repeat, is wholly apart from me and in front of me, the world of mystery is a place where I find myself committed, and, I would add, not partially committed, not committed in regard to some determinate and specialized aspect of myself, but committed as a whole man in so far as I achieve a unity which, for that matter, by its very definition, can never be grasped in itself, grasped as something apart from me; this unity is not an object of knowledge but of my creative impulse and my faith. As soon as we postulate the notion of mystery, we abolish that frontier between what lies in the self and what lies before the self, a frontier which, as we saw just now, could be thrust back or restored to a former position, but without ever ceasing to reconstitute itself at every moment of reflection.

The first example of mystery that I gave in this book was the mystery of evil, and that is, I think, one of the most significant examples we could choose. I make evil problematical when I treat it as a kind of breakdown that might happen in a piece of machinery, or as something lacking, or as a functional failure. Evil reveals itself to me as, on the contrary, a mystery when I have recognized that I cannot treat myself as something external to evil, as simply having to observe evil from the outside and map out its contours, but that on the contrary I am implicated in evil—just as one is implicated, for instance, in some crime. Evil is not only in front of my eyes, it is within me: even more than this, in such a realm the distinction between what is within me and what lies outside me becomes meaningless; one might say that such a distinction has a physical rather than a metaphysical validity. One could think of many other examples; thus it could be shown that there is a mystery of love, just as there is a mystery of knowledge, and that the mystery of love—in reality a mystery of incarnation—specifies itself in innumerable forms; that is why I have been able to deal, in one of my books, with the mystery of the family, and to show that one remains at a level below the intimate reality of that mystery so long as one is imprisoned by the categories imposed by the problematical approach.

But how can we recognize mystery? Only by means of a kind of inner grip that is nothing other than an ingatheredness. For my own part, I am careful, here, to avoid speaking of intuition. For this regrasping of oneself, this inner grip, which I am speaking of, is quite certainly not a way of looking at something outside; it is rather a kind of concentration and, as it were, inner reflection. But we can see immediately that the recognition of a mystery demands an approach which is quite the contrary of that demanded by the solution of a problem; to solve a problem, the mind must turn outside itself, it must fling itself on the elements with which it must work. One should add that this inner grasp or grip seems always to have the aspect of an easing of tension, of a letting go, and not of a willed tensing-up of oneself. But we also ought to make it clear that this easing of tension, this letting go, is not a state of relaxedness. Unless I am very much deceived, we must carefully distinguish *Entspannung* and *Auflosung:* for it does seem that allowing oneself to go slack inside is always the beginning of a kind of dissolution; the easing of tension of which we are speaking here has its basis in consent or assent (*Zustimmung*). I ought to say in passing that the relationship that binds man's freedom and God's grace can be disengaged only by a philosophy of consent—and, what is more, that both freedom and grace can only be, I will not say understood, but recognized and affirmed on the basis of such a mediating philosophy.

The above observations, far from being foreign to the question we started with at the beginning of this chapter, in fact directly suggest our answer to it. The inroads made in our time by techniques cannot fail to imply for man the obliteration, the progressive effacement, of this world of mystery which is at one a world of presences and of hope; it is not sufficient merely to say that, at the level of mystery, man's desires and fears, which lie behind his technical achievements, are lifted up beyond any assignable limit; we must add that human nature is tending to become more and more incapable of raising itself above desire and fear in their ordinary state, and of reaching in prayer or contemplation a state that transcends all earthly vicissitudes. And the word 'earthly' here is significant and revealing. It could be claimed that the perfecting of techniques is to all appearances making man more and more earthly; and we should note also that the more man becomes, as it were, riveted to the earth, the more he will be led to multiply and perfect the techniques which allow him to assure his grip on earth and, so to say, to assert his establishment there. Yet there is a paradox here on which we can profitably linger.

Can we really say, in fact, that technical man is becoming more and more strongly rooted in the earth? It does not seem so. Rootedness seems to imply a grafting on to the local scene, a local individuality of custom, which, as we have already observed, technical progress tends to forbid or at least to fight against with growing success. But ought we not to ask ourselves whether, in fact, the love of life in the deepest sense is not always linked to this grafting, this individuality? And, in fact, everything seems to show that life in our time is less and less loved, is more and more despised. Following out this line of thought, we should be forced to ask ourselves whether technical progress does not run the risk of having, as one of its consequences, a kind of return to nomadism; one can observe something of this sort among many unskilled labourers who, in fact, take root nowhere and carry with them wherever they go an all too understandable resentment against their growingly inhuman conditions of life.

When we develop some of the remarks we have made in this chapter, we shall be led to believe that the excessive development of techniques in our time is tending to superimpose on life, and in a certain sense to substitute for life, an almost entirely factitious superstructure; yet this superstructure is becoming for men in general the familiar background that they cannot do without. That would be the deeper meaning of the exodus from the country towards the towns. It is quite clear that what attracts the agricultural labourer in town existence is something that has almost no relationship with what has been traditionally considered as 'life'.

This loss of feeling for living reality is certainly one of the deeper underlying causes of that of all in the birth-rate which can be observed in all countries of so-called 'advanced' civilization. If we want to understand the psychology of very many contemporaries of ours, and in particular if we want to understand the kind of crisis which has overtaken the relationship between the older and the younger generation, we have to take note of the fact that life is being less and less felt as a gift to be handed on, and more and more felt as a kind of incomprehensible calamity, like a flood, against which we ought to be able to build dykes. There is nothing really ridiculous in the assertion that the growingly general use of techniques of birth-prevention is only one aspect of a very widespread impingement of techniques upon realms from which, until recently, they were almost shut out.

But we can see at once *that a technical world, with its compass set in such a direction, can only end in despair*. For, by the very nature of such a world, it can offer us no possibility of help where techniques are useless—as primarily, and above all, they are useless, of course, in the presence of death. How, from the point of view of such a world, could death appear as anything else than the flinging on the scrap heap of a being that has ceased to be of service—and that no longer *is* anything, the moment it is no longer *of any use*? But here, it seems to me, we are at the nub of our argument. We have reached a point where it becomes possible to understand how techniques, which, to start with, seemed to us neutral in relation to human values, can become techniques *of* sin and *for* sin—techniques at the service of sin.

Quite generally, we can in fact say that the development of techniques does inevitably tend to give a primacy, at the practical level, to the idea of output. Given these conditions, a being whose output has fallen below a certain level and become practically nil will, from the point of view of a world in which technique rules, a technocratic world, be regarded as an unprofitable charge on the society which still feels itself bound to care for and maintain him. And the phrase 'care and maintenance', which is used of machinery, is very revealing in this new context. Man is thought of on the model of a machine, on the model of a mere physical object—since in fact he is being treated as if he *were* a mere physical object. And it is perhaps through this tendency to treat man as a machine that one can best detect the scope and purpose of materialism as a practical philosophy. A materialistic philosophy was able, during the eighteenth and nineteenth centuries, to gain adherents among men of simple and at bottom idealistic temperament who believed that materialism was true, but who very seldom thought of drawing any practical corollaries from it about the treatment of human beings. I have no doubt that there were many 'materialists' in the last century who accepted an ethical rigorism rather like that of Kant—even though, from a strictly logical point of view, such a mixture is the height of absurdity. Materialism did not become a real force, it did not assume its true dimensions, until it became a coherent attitude towards human beings. And one must note, in passing, that this 'materialistic' attitude towards human beings, this tendency to treat man as a machine, has often in the past been that of individuals and sometimes of whole social groups, who believed that they accepted a spiritual and even a religious conception of the universe, but nevertheless continued to treat whole wide classes of their fellow-beings as mere instruments, whose output was all that mattered. In this, there was a frightful failure to draw the obvious conclusions from accepted premisses, of which men have very slowly become aware, and which is still very far from having produced all the ill effects that are latent in it. But it seems to me that to-day this double dissociation, of spiritual premisses from spiritual conclusions, and of materialistic premisses from materialistic conclusions, is coming to an end. One of the things I mean by that is that the inhuman consequences of a systematically materialist mode of thinking are to-day obvious to everyone. I am thinking now, of course of the reduction of multitudes of human beings to a condition of slavery, in which their status as human beings is almost refused recognition; but there is another side to the picture, and when I speak of this double dissociation coming to an end, I have in mind the fact that a kind of Christianity which does not express itself in a persevering effort to procure decent conditions of life for those who are still plunged in wretchedness must seem to us as if infected at its heart by a principle of falsehood and death.

Thus we are to-day facing a much clearer situation, one with which our powers of reflective thought can hardly fail to get to grips. From the point of view of modern materialism, a practice which the rest of us rightly judge as monstrously inhuman, such as the methodical extermination of the incurably ill, seems to correspond to a logic which is not only strict but unanswerable. We may say the same of the extermination in wartime of slaves who have reached such a degree of exhaustion that they can no longer earn their keep, however wretched a keep that may be. As I said at the beginning of this chapter, such proceedings do still, thank God, arouse general indignation. But one may fear that, if this is so, it is only because men are not yet sufficiently adapted to a merely technical world; and we have to recognize that we are already well on the road that leads to the most frightful type of barbarism, a barbarism based on reason.

The postulate in the name of which such excesses can be condemned is that of the existence, at the very heart of the world of mere problems with which technical thinking deals, of a mystery of being, a mystery which is irreducible and inviolable. However, we must be careful not to fall here into the errors of the agnosticism of the last century. There can certainly be no question of assimilating the notion of mystery to that of some sort of element of brute fact which remains opaque to thought; on the contrary, thought, if it is to raise itself above modes of activity that are below its proper scope, cannot fail to recognize in mystery its own source and its own homeland.

From this point of view, the superiority of our own historical period to those which preceded it rests perhaps, as I indicated a moment ago, in the fact that those equivocations, with which such a great number of free-thinkers and also of believers remained satisfied for so long, can no longer stand up to the attack of reflective criticism. We are proceeding in a direct road towards the laying utterly bare of our human condition and all its implications. But the very note of our human condition is, in fact, that it is not assimilable to some kind of objective and already existing structure which we have merely to uncover and explore. The human condition, whatever may be the foundations on which it ultimately rests, seems to be in some ways dependent on the very manner in which it is understood. In our own time, a philosopher like Heidegger seems to me to have grasped and expressed this in a wonderfully clear and definite way. But it is also becoming more and more obvious that when man seeks to understand his condition by using as his model the products of his own technical skill, he infinitely degrades himself and condemns himself to deny, that is, in the end, to destroy, those deep and basic sentiments which for thousands of years have guided his conduct. Obviously, in such a process of denial and destruction, there is nothing which is absurd or contradictory at a merely logical level. But does not the proper function and dignity of philosophy consist in recognizing that this logic of negation and death, far from being obviously true, on the contrary bears witness against itself when confronted by a more enlightened exercise of reason, of a kind that has taken care not to break the ties that attach man's reason to a wider protective reality, enveloping it on all sides?

It is, in fact, from this extremely general and even metaphysical point of view that the problem of the relationships between technical progress and sin should be envisaged. Broadly, we might say that man's increasing mastery over nature has been accompanied, for reasons which I have already partially indicated, by a more and more complete capitulation of man before his own fears and desires, or even before the ungovernable element in his nature. Man's mastery of nature, then, is a mastery which has less and less control over *itself*. And the best piece of evidence we can offer that man is becoming more and more incapable of ruling over nature is that he tends to think less and less of what legitimate claim he can have to exercise such a sovereignty. In the last resort, it seems to him too obvious to be worth insisting on that his qualification for this cosmic regency lies in those intellectual faculties which have, in fact, permitted him to develop his science and his techniques to their present point of perfection.

But here we come again on that age-old notion of sin, as that notion has been understood by all the great religious traditions without exception; I mean sin as pride, sin as *hubris*, sin, ultimately, as revolt. And I feel inclined to ask myself whether the excessive development of techniques during the last century has not tended to constitute something which we should have to call a *body of sin*, in contrast to that *body of light* whose sole principle is charity. The tragic problem confronting man to-day is that of knowing whether he will have to bear onward this body of sin, hoisted like a burden on his shoulders, till he begins to confuse this heavy load with himself and must face those reprisals which a spirit of unmeasure and presumption will undoubtedly call down on him.

It would be pointless to attempt to disguise the fact that, uttered at this time and place, such words have a futile and ridiculous air: what chance have they of being understood or even attended to? And yet the spectacle of powerlessness and confusion which is presented to us by those who fancy they have been made responsible for the destiny of our planet has about it, in so far as it goes, something comforting. We can ask ourselves whether, from the moment in which the representatives of the peoples, or those who appropriate that title, show themselves so sadly incapable of accomplishing their tasks, it does not become incumbent on those who have neither been given any power nor delegated any authority to prepare, among the shades and the clarities of the realm of meditation, a more acceptable and less inhuman future. Here, certainly, more than anywhere else, we must be cautious and humble; we must forbid ourselves large and vague more or less utopian ambitions, of the sort expressed in the aspirations with which international congresses generally draw to a close. Here again it is in our own ingatheredness, and in that only, that we can find a place of refuge; I speak of ingatheredness or recollection here, rather than of prayer, just because the word 'prayer' has certain ambiguous overtones which, I imagine, many men of noble spirit still find uncongenial. But I do affirm that it is through ingatheredness only, through recollection in the highest sense of that word, through a concentrated recalling of ourselves to ourselves, that those powers of love and humility can be born and can be grouped in strength, which alone, in the long run, can form an adequate counterpoise to the blind, and blinding, pride of the technician, closed in by his techniques.

PART TWO

CHAPTER I

THE PHILOSOPHER & THE CONTEMPORARY WORLD

IN all ages, there has been a tendency to emphasize the dubious or risky role of the philosopher in relation to society in general. It does very much seem as if the philosopher had not such deep roots in the world as the average man, even if it is no longer possible for him to detach himself from the world in the fashion of a pure contemplative withdrawn to a hermit's solitude.

The other side of the picture is that the world, for its part, either refuses to recognize the importance of the philosopher and treats him as a figure of comedy—or, on the other hand, if it does take a philosopher up, works unwearyingly to distort his message and, if I dare put it so, to degrade his proper nature.

These are very general remarks, by way of preliminary. It is not my purpose to remain at the level of such abstractions as '*the* philosopher' and '*the* world': on the contrary, I am setting out, if not to solve, at least to state, certain difficult and vexatious problems that have to do with our actual contemporary world, the world that we have to live in even if it disgusts us in so many ways, the world from which we have no right merely to turn aside; for if we do turn aside from it, we are guilty of a sort of desertion.

We ought to notice, in the first place, that our idea of what a philosopher is has, if we compare it to the ancient idea of a philosopher, suffered in modern times and above all in contemporary times a real degradation; it has been degraded in the same degree to which the notion of wisdom, of *sophia*, has lost, if not its meaning, at least its original power of inspiring veneration. In the last century, the practising philosopher was in the majority of cases reduced to becoming a mere professor of philosophy; this to the horror and indignation of the most free and lucid spirits of that time, such as Nietzsche and Schopenhauer. The professor of philosophy is too often a specialist in some degree intoxicated by his own speciality, who expounds to his students or sometimes to a rather wider public either his system, if by good luck he has one, or else a kind of blending and distillation of other men's systems, or else, what is certainly less compromising, a history of the systems that have preceded his own. One ought also to add, and this point is more important than on the surface it might appear to be, that in many countries, and more particularly in France, the professor of philosophy is liable literally to succumb under the burden of tasks connected with his post which have no specific connection with philosophy, but which have to do with helping an enormous number of students to prepare for and pass examinations.

Under such conditions, it may be said that even the head of a university department who does genuinely remain a philosopher—who retains, I mean, his power of meditation or, at a deeper level still, what one might call his intellectual virginity—can only succeed in doing so at the price of an effort which is literally heroic, and on condition that he leads an almost ascetic life. But such an asceticism, admirable in itself, inevitably exacts a price. The philosopher runs the risk of cutting himself off, in some sense, from life, and of little by little, without being aware of it, substituting for life a realm of thought which is quite his own, a sort of closed and well cared-for garden whose shrubs and bushes he expertly lops and prunes. It may be agreed that there goes with this intellectual horticulture a certain sense of inner freedom: but is such a freedom really very different from that which has been known and enjoyed by prisoners in actual prisons of iron and stone?

From another point of view, it is obvious that so soon as philosophy is conceived in this fashion, as a neat enclosed terrain, its possibilities of working fruitfully outwards are very much reduced. The philosopher confines himself to looking after a certain piece of property in which he takes, we may say, delight; but he is in danger in very many cases of considering, if not with hostility, at least with distrust, those whom we are forced to call his competitors. Of course, there are large-hearted exceptions. But the danger is there, and it is not one to be underestimated. And this is the source of that feeling of discomfort and sometimes of actual disquiet with which one finds oneself considering these peasant-proprietors in the philosophical domain, and their type of activity. On the one hand, nobody could fail to admire their seriousness, their honesty, their disinterestedness, for nothing has a smaller sales-value than philosophy understood in this sense, and if I spoke of the fear of competition felt by such philosophers just now, I was not speaking in commercial terms. On the other hand, how can we fail to be alarmed by the limited and abstruse nature of such a type of research? Nevertheless, we ought at once to add that the philosopher who, in the precisely contrary case, seeks out huge audiences, multiplies his impact by means of the press and the radio, and plays, if I dare put it so, the part of a little Jack Horner with a finger in every pie, though he avoids the particular kind of shipwreck I have just been dealing with, in compensation runs the risk of betraying, in the most serious fashion, his fundamental vocation. The profound reflections of Plato on the dangers of flattery, of *kolakeia*, have not lost any contemporary point. There is a general modern phenomenon of mental masochism, whose causes we ought to be able to lay bare; because of this masochism, a growing number of individuals feel a periodical need to be outraged—not in their convictions, that would be too strong a word for the type of mentality I am thinking of, but in their habitual attitudes. A philosopher who is so very well known that it is unnecessary to name him here was playing up to this attitude when he said to the journalists who had gathered to receive him on a Swiss airfield, as soon as he got out of his plane: 'Gentlemen, God is dead!' That is a very striking example of the kind of flattery, under the mask of provocation, which I have just been speaking of.

I should like to linger for a moment over this anecdote. Let us leave aside the question of what ultimate judgment we ought to bring to bear on Nietzsche's tragic and prophetic affirmation. What is clear is that as soon as Nietzsche's affirmation, 'God is dead', is blared forth to journalists, or is put forward as a possible sensational headline, it becomes degraded, not only in the sense of losing, in this new context, all real meaning, but in the sense of becoming an absurd parody of its original self. There is an existential difference between Nietzsche's sigh or sob and this sort of publicity hand-out, obviously intended to make a cheap sensation: 'Gentleman, I have a piece of news for you. God has been liquidated. Isn't that something?'

But at the same time we must recognize, not without the deepest anguish, that invitations to the philosopher to conduct himself in this degrading fashion are piling up on every side. So soon as the philosopher consents to be taken in charge by publicity agents, by impresarios, he negates his own function and vocation as a philosopher. It is also, of course, quite natural that the philosopher's desire for publicity should manifest itself more and more in the outward guise of a wish to shock. Let us add that, to the thinker who desires above all to oppose *bourgeois* convictions, this wish to shock will appear as a manifestation of the revolutionary spirit. The effort which certain circles have made to revive interest in the unreadable and rightly infamous works of the Marquis de Sade is a case in point. Let us note also, in passing, that the true revolutionary is quite within his rights in reminding us that a certain sort of anti-*bourgeois* literary attitude may itself be merely a *bourgeois* phenomenon.

Obviously, we have only to consider such attitudes and their outward manifestations to return with increased sympathy and respect towards the notion of the philosopher as an ascetic. But we still feel certain qualms about this notion, and again it is important to make their nature clear.

There has recently been republished in France Maurice Blondel's famous thesis of 1893, *L'Action*, which formerly gave rise to such regrettable misunderstandings and which remains nevertheless one of the great speculative works in the French language. There have also been recently reprinted certain admirable lectures by Jules Lagneau, who was Alain's teacher, and who himself remains a first-rate example of the pure philosopher in France. Now, if we go back in our imagination to the distant period when these lectures were first delivered and when *L'Action* first appeared, we cannot help noticing that that was a world at peace, a world not weighed down by the terrible threats which we, for our part, know only too intimately. In such a world of peace, the attitude of such thinkers, the whole bent of whose nature turned them towards the deepest and most genuine research, was not merely justified; it was the only attitude that could be described as genuinely philosophical. But it does seem to me that things are by no means the same to-day, and that to-day the philosopher has to take a definite stand in regard to the wretchedness of a world whose complete destruction is not inconceivable. For my own part, I have frankly the conviction that we are in a situation without precedent, which I would define very briefly by saying that suicide has become possible on a mankind-wide scale. It is impossible to think out this situation, without becoming aware that each of us is at almost every moment in the presence of a radical choice, and contributes by what he thinks, by what he does, by what he is, either to increase or on the contrary to lessen the likelihood of such a world-scale suicide. But it is obvious also that it is only at the philosophical level that the essential nature of this choice can be made clear.

To round off these considerations, I should notice that there is still another temptation to which, in fact, contemporary philosophers do frequently yield. There is a danger of the philosopher taking his stand, much too hastily, on paper rather than in reality, and most frequently by appending his signature to some manifesto, about matters of which he has only a superficial knowledge, a hearsay knowledge which is in reality mere ignorance. I will take a specific example again here, that of a petition signed by a number of intellectuals who demanded that the United Nations Assembly should provide a seat for the Government of Communist China. They failed to see that the problem was in the first place one of *opportuneness*, and as such not one on which any of the signatories were in a position to pronounce.

One can think of many other examples of the same sort. The error here consists, also, invariably of first postulating certain general principles in a quite abstract fashion and then declaring hastily that in such or such a concrete case these principles imply such and such a definite practical decision. But, leaving aside the fact that it is sometimes not allowable to postulate such principles as valid in all imaginable cases whatsoever, it very often happens that the particular case to which they are being applied is too imperfectly known, in its particularity and concrete connections, for any such inference from the abstract general principle to the particular decision to be allowable. A good example of this is to be found in the extraordinary rashness with which some French intellectuals have been demanding the immediate evacuation of Indo-China. They start from the idea that colonialism is incompatible with the general notion they have formed of the rights of man. But, quite aside from the fact that their idea of colonialism is much too summary and simplified, and from the fact that in some ways a colonizing power can have a beneficial effect on the colonial peoples themselves, the whole problem lay in knowing whether on the one hand such an evacuation was practically possible, and on the other hand, supposing it were practically possible, whether its effect would not be to deliver the colonial peoples themselves over to the terroristic action of armed groups at the service of Soviet imperialism. In a situation of this sort, everything is involved in almost inextricable complexity, and to formulate imperatives dictated by ignorance, and in many cases by political sectarianism, is to betray the inescapable demands of straight thinking.

Thus the very first duty of a philosopher is to have a clear sense of the limits of his own knowledge and to recognize that there are realms in which his lack of competence to make judgments is complete. Or, in other words, we may say that the philosopher should be perpetually on guard against making false claims that are incompatible with his true vocation.

Proudhon used to say: 'Intellectuals are frivolous', and unfortunately this is terribly true, the deep reason for it being that the intellectual has not to deal, as the peasant and the workman have, with a tangible and stubborn reality, a reality which resists fantasies; the intellectual works with words, and paper permits absolutely anything to be written on it. Of this particular danger the intellectuals of our day ought to be continually aware. Proudhon used to add that, if intellectuals are frivolous, the people is serious. This, unfortunately, is perhaps no longer true to-day—because of the press and the radio, which have almost invariably a corrupting effect. The people remains serious only on condition of remaining itself, and we must recognize that this is becoming a more and more infrequent case, because of a certain diffusion of *bourgeois* standards whose results are, in some respects, melancholy and regrettable. In some respects, I say: from another point of view, this diffusion of *bourgeois* standards is a desirable thing, especially in so far as it corresponds to a genuine improvement of living conditions among the peasants and workers. One is in the presence there of a sort of tragic antinomy (material improvement going hand in hand with moral decay) which it is hard to see how to surmount.

It may be objected that to deny the philosopher the right to take a definite stand on concrete political issues is at bottom a hypocritical way of inviting him not to commit himself, to remain at the level of assertions of general principle. But that is not what I am aiming at. I will take two examples which should make my drift clearer. I should not hesitate to say that in a country in which the same people are persecuted for racial or religious reasons, it is the philosopher's duty to commit himself utterly, however many risks he may run, by making his protest. Silence in such a case is complicity. But in this case nobody could claim that the persecutor has a better knowledge of his special subject than the philosopher. It is even the very opposite that is true. The anti-semite is not better informed about the Jews than the man who fights anti-semitism. In fact, what is at issue here is not knowledge at all but ignorant prejudice, which it is the philosopher's duty to attack. We may say that principle intervenes directly here, in all its sublime irreducibility.

Let me take another example: I personally hold that the philosopher, as such, was bound to protest against the way in which the purge was carried out in France after the war, by men who, often unjustly, claimed to incarnate the Resistance, this at a moment when, the war being at an end, the word 'Resistance' was losing all real meaning. That it was permissible to set up irregular courts, to allow victims the right to judge their persecutors just *because* of the spirit of vindictiveness that inspired them—all this the philosopher was in duty bound to deny, as forcibly as possible. Here again the principle at stake was glaringly obvious.

But it goes without saying that these two examples which I have just cited have something in common. In both cases, we have to do with fanaticism. For, in fact—and I assert this without a shadow of hesitation—the first duty of the philosopher in our world to-day is to fight against fanaticism *under whatever guise it may appear.*

Jules Lagneau, whose recently republished lectures I mentioned a short time ago, expressed his views on fanaticism in the following words: 'In defining our thought, and in putting it into precise formulations, we shall take care not to become shut up within ourselves. We shall remember that slavery to words lies at the roots of fanaticism, and that, if fanaticism destroys liberty, it is because fanaticism arises from this servitude. We shall remember that ideas retain their proper life only if the mind keeps them alive by perpetually judging them, that is to say by perpetually keeping its own place at a level above them, and that ideas cease to be good, cease even to be ideas, when they cease to be at once the solid seat and the active expression of our inner freedom. Fanaticism, then, will be foreign to us, it is the enemy, and we are not going to go over to the enemy; it is evil, we shall not sow it, but we shall sow that which we wish to reap. We shall act with calm and constancy in the world around us, showing in our everyday life the spirit that works within us and opposing ourselves to every spirit that is not entirely reasonable and entirely generous. But we shall sympathize actively with whatever is done, in any political party, in any church, in accordance with this spirit of pure reason and pure generosity, without fearing the increasing strength that may thus accrue to that party or church. It is a matter of little importance to us through whom truth sees the light of day, through whom salvation comes'.

These memorable lines are taken from the 'Simple Notes for a Programme of Union and Action' which were drafted in 1892 and were to become the charter of the Union for Moral Action. I remember that at the beginning of this century the latter changed its name, became the Union for Truth and that, little by little, under political influence, its character appreciably deteriorated.

But what matters here is Lagneau's perfectly clear vision of the philosopher's function, one of the most high and pure conceptions of that function, without any doubt, of our time. Even to-day, it is a view and a conception that imposes itself on the attention and respect of men of good will. I am not digressing from my subject here, for the philosopher denies his proper role if he fails to make the preliminary assertion that he is a man of good will. I am not taking that phrase in the rather indefinite sense which Jules Romains gives to it in his long novel, but in the sense of the Gospels, a sense for which the notion of good will almost merges with that of a methodical love of peace, and I am not thinking here only of peace between the nations, but, just as much if not more, of the peace that can reign in that inner city which I form with myself and my neighbour.

Subsequent events have given a more complete confirmation than anyone at the time could have expected of Lagneau's profound thought that, at the root of fanaticism, lies man's servitude to words. And I would say that the first mission of the philosopher, in this world or in opposition to this world, is to refuse to accept that servitude. Among French thinkers, Brice Parain has demonstrated with extreme clarity that the problem of language is in itself a metaphysical problem; and this is what Heidegger also proclaims in his letter on humanism, when he says that language is the dwelling place of being, a fact which confers upon language a certain quality of sacredness. As far as Heidegger is concerned, however, I should note in passing that he himself risks damaging this special quality of language, in so far as he does violence to language, in not hesitating to coin words of which one doubts that they will ever receive that patina which comes from constant use by many people over a long period of time. For my part, I hold on the contrary, with Bergson, that it is essential to avoid neologisms; I think that philosophers ought not only to come back to the simplest words, but that they should give these words a higher value by removing, as it were, the layers of grease with which they have become covered by impropriety in common speech.

Here we are coming close to the method of Plato in his dialogues. But it is clear that reflection on the meanings of words must be directed, just as Plato wanted it to be, towards a grasp of what traditional philosophers used to call *essences*. One cannot protest too strongly against a kind of existentialism, or a kind of caricature of existentialism, which claims to deprive the notion of essence of its old value and to allow it only a subordinate position. But this does not mean that the notion of essence does not need to be thought out again, on the basis of a philosophy which affirms the primacy of a kind of subjectivity, or more exactly of a kind of intersubjectivity, whose rights the philosophy of the schools has too often failed to recognize.

Nevertheless, when we agree that philosophy should turn towards essences, are we not inviting it to commit itself to a road that leads out of our actual world and can only end in some realm of intelligibles? Does philosophy, conceived in this way, not run the risk of becoming a way of escape? In other words have we not come back to the point we made earlier, about the danger of philosophy becoming a sort of enclosed garden?

We are on difficult and shifting ground here, and we must see if we can manage to state this problem as distinctly as possible. No philosopher would be willing to accept the idea of philosophy as a way of escape, but might there not be a question of the philosopher being in duty bound to refuse to accept a world, like our real world here, of disorder and crime where the values of the mind and spirit can no longer find a home?

However, what do I mean by the philosopher's *refusal* to accept this world? One can imagine the possibility of an attitude of refusal in the world of action; such an attitude might be expressed, for instance, by the rejection of techniques. And we can imagine a sort of philosophical Ghandi-ism. But is it really the duty of the philosopher to create for himself a framework of existence as foreign as possible to the general conditions of contemporary life? It would be rash and even absurd to claim that this really is one of his duties. For in the limiting case we should have to acknowledge that the philosopher ought to lead the life of a hermit or of an Indian guru. But such a life implies a particular vocation, an essentially mystical vocation, which we ought certainly not to confuse with the vocation of the philosopher.

Must we say then that the attitude of refusal we are thinking of operates only on the plane of pure theory? Such a theoretical attitude of refusal is expressed, for instance, in a philosophy of the absurd, such as Albert Camus has attempted to define in his *Mythe de Sisyphe*. We are here at the very core of the problem with which I have been wishing to deal. But, even in relation to this philosophy of the absurd, the questions we want to ask come under two headings. First, we must ask whether any philosopher is really qualified to pass the verdict on the universe, that the universe is absurd. Secondly, admitting for the sake of argument that such a verdict can be legitimately passed, we must ask ourselves what practical consequences such a verdict entails: what does it imply that we should do?

It is important here to notice that the question under discussion is that of the absurdity of the universe taken as a whole, not merely the absurdity of our own historic human world, an absurdity for which one would, at first glance, be tempted to declare men themselves responsible. For a sensitive conscience like that of Albert Camus the existence of undeserved suffering (the suffering of children, for instance, and that due to accidents considered as things that happen gratuitously) forbids an honourable thinker to allow either that the world can be the work of God or can even, in the full sense of the word, be an intelligible world. One might add, I think, that from a point of view like that of Camus the contemporary horrors we are witnessing must spring from a rooted irrationality at the very depth of things. A stand like that of Camus, whatever we may think of it at a metaphysical level, has undoubtedly a certain moral validity: it is honest and honourable, the stand of a man who does not want to let himself be imposed on, and who refuses from the very depths of his being to confuse what he desires with what actually exists.

But at the same time I should add that this attitude of Camus is also extremely simple-minded. It is that of a man who has never reached the stage of what I have often called *secondary reflection*. There is a fundamental question which Camus never seems to have put to himself: by what right am I qualified to pass this sort of verdict on the world? Of two things, one:—either I myself do not belong to the world under discussion, but in that case have I not every reason to suppose that it is impenetrable to me and that I am not qualified to judge its value—or, on the other hand, I really am part of the world, and if the world is absurd, so am I absurd, too. Camus, perhaps, might concede this. It is, however, a destructive concession. Again, of two things, one: either I am myself absurd in my ultimate nature—in which case so are my judgments absurd, they negate themselves, it cannot be conceded that they have any sort of validity—or, on the other hand, we have to admit that I have a double nature, that there is a part of me which is not absurd and which can make valid judgments about absurdity: but how did this aspect of me which is not absurd get there? I cannot even admit the possibility of its existence without beginning to formulate a kind of dualism which, in some sense, splits my original assertion of the *total* absurdity of the universe apart.

All this could be demonstrated in another, and briefer, fashion. There is no point in saying that the universe is absurd unless I can compare the universe with some idea of order or rationality to which I observe that it does not conform: but how did I come to be aware of this ideal? Where did I get the notion from?

All this amounts to saying that as soon as I begin to reflect on a position like that of Camus, I am inevitably led to substitute for his philosophy of the absurd either a gnosticism for which the coming into existence of the universe is a kind of fall or a simple manichean dualism of embattled good and evil. Faced with these two possible developments of Camus's attitude, what, in turn, would be the attitude of the philosopher, as such? I say 'as such' deliberately. We must not bring in here the religious beliefs which a philosopher might privately hold, if, *as well as* being a philosopher, he were also, for instance, a Roman Catholic. The problem that we are discussing has no meaning at all unless we consider the philosopher either as a non-believer or as a man who, when he sets himself to philosophizing, puts his private religious beliefs aside.

Before I attempt to work out a rudimentary answer to this question, it might be useful to revert to the second of the two headings under which I put the questions we want to ask about an attitude like that of Camus: allowing for the sake of argument that the philosopher may have the right to pass the verdict that the universe is absurd, what practical consequences does such a verdict entail—what does it imply that we should do? It seems obvious to me that the implications for action of this attitude are of an almost completely indeterminate sort. On the one hand, we can imagine a philosopher of cynical temperament who will see in the world he condemns for its absurdity a mere object of derision, in so far as he does not merely turn away from that world in disdain, seeking to make his private life as pleasant as possible. One can also imagine a man who, through a certain remnant of magnanimity, seeks in each particular case to denounce injustices and abuses or to struggle against such natural scourges as disease, without however having any very ambitious illusions about the scope and importance of the results he is likely to achieve. At a first glance, we might be tempted to think this second attitude less logical than the first one. For what is this magnanimity? Where does it come from? How can we attempt to justify its existence or its function in a world given over to absurdity? Here we have a striking practical example of that simple manichean dualism of which I was just speaking. On the other hand, the first attitude, that of the cynic, if it is superficially coherent, implies also the negation of what has been traditionally understood by the word 'philosophy': it is not only a suicide of thought, it is the most ignoble sort of suicide imaginable.

This leads us back, by a roundabout way, to our fundamental question: what attitude the philosopher, as such, ought to take up when faced by the temptations of a neo-gnosticism and a neo-manicheism, temptations which, it must be recognized are, in such a world as ours, in danger of becoming irresistible for an increasing number of persons? This may even be true, in spite of superficial appearances, in the world that owes allegiance to the Soviets. Somebody was telling me the other day of a sect which had arisen in Russia, a few months ago, in the depths of a desolate countryside. Under what influence it would be hard to say, the villagers had discovered that they ought to sacrifice everything to an inner purification, at the end of which they would be snatched away from this world of perdition and lifted up to the third heaven. They had forbidden their children to go to school, for everything that was taught there came from the devil. Warned of all this, the authorities intervened and sought without success to din into the misguided peasants the elements of the materialist catechism. It all ended with deportations. But it did seem as if, throughout the neighbourhood, this mysterious flame was likely to propagate itself in a dangerous fashion. This anecdote does not illustrate merely the difficulties which the authorities are likely to come up against in their crazy effort to root out all religion from the soul of the Russian people. One may also conceive that the general flatness of contemporary rationalism, so thoroughly opposed to the deepest aspirations of the human soul, is likely sooner or later to provoke more or less analogous reactions even among more 'evolved' peoples.

All this is only a digression in appearance: I believe I am not mistaken in holding that this devastated world of ours is constituting a more and more favourable field for the resurgence of a kind of dualism which modern philosophy—I am thinking chiefly of German idealism—had claimed to exorcize. From the strictly philosophic point of view, are we to see all this as a *mere* temptation? To use that word as I have used it is already to take one's stand, it is to say implicitly that a philosopher conscious of his responsibilities can only reject dualism. However, let us be careful here. It is obvious that from the point of view of orthodox Christianity this dualism, whether or not it asserts itself in expressly manichean forms, is something that must be rejected. But one has perhaps not the right to postulate *a priori* a necessary agreement between the demands of philosophy as such and the affirmations of Christian doctrine, as such. What I mean is that even if, as I personally believe, such an agreement between true philosophy and true doctrine does ultimately exist, its existence, nevertheless, can certainly not be laid down as an axiom. In a quite other direction, we should also take wary notice of the fact that, if the kind of neo-dualism we are discussing is incompatible with an organic—or to be franker, with an academic—notion of philosophy as a unified system, that notion itself ought no longer to be accepted without examination: as for such a long time it was in France, particularly by those philosophers, of the academic type, whom I mentioned earlier.

These, however, are all preliminary observations. Let us try, now, to get to the heart of the problem. In the first place, let us remind ourselves that to-day there can be no philosophy worth considering that will not involve an analysis, of a phenomenological type, bearing on the fundamental situation of man. More clearly than their predecessors saw it, this has been seen especially by the best contemporary German philosophers, of whom one would mention first Scheler and next Landsberg, but also Jaspers and Heidegger. In the context of the work of such men, it appears to-day to be a fact beyond discussion that what is proper to man, in so far as he merely lives his life without also straining to think out his life, is to be in a situation; while for the philosopher, who, for his part, intends to think out both his own life and life in general, the essential task is to recognize, and also to make a reconnaissance of, this human situation, to explore it as thoroughly as possible; without, however, at any time hoping to be able to acquire that exhaustive knowledge of it to which the objects that science studies so readily lend themselves. The very idea of such exhaustive, objective knowledge is in this context a contradictory one: to recognize, and to make reconnaissances, is not the same sort of thing as finally and exhaustively *to know*.

From this point of view, it is easy to understand that the philosopher is at once *in* the world and *out of* the world, and that this paradoxical duality is involved in this very status as philosopher; this, moreover, is true not only of the qualified professional philosopher, but of anyone who strives to adopt a philosophic attitude.

There have certainly been periods during which this duality was not so clearly and so painfully experienced as it perhaps is to-day; and I would add that this duality does invariably tend to efface itself from the consciousness of the academic type of philosopher, for whom his own system tends to become a substitute for the world and for life.

But the more clearly this duality is present to one's consciousness, the more one is forced to recognize the impossibility, for that consciousness, of adhering to any kind of pantheistic philosophy, properly so called. From the point of view of this duality, pantheism implies what one might describe as a fraudulent or illicit notion of the idea of totality. In the last analysis there can be no whole without a thought which grasps it as a whole; and this grasping of what is before the mind as a whole can be effected only by a sort of voluntary halt in a kind of progressive movement of thought. When a neo-Hegelian philosopher, like Bradley in England, postulates an Absolute which gathers into itself, though not without transforming them, all the appearances of which the finite mind must remain the prisoner, he seems to me to fail to realize the basic fact that the act of inclusion can never be more than partial, that it remains always linked to a kind of onward journey of thought, so that we really do not know what we are saying when we speak of an absolute inclusion. But there can be no pantheism without the idea of such an absolute, or complete and final, inclusion: that is to say without passing to a limiting case which reflection cannot fail to pronounce as being arbitrarily and illegitimately postulated. This, probably, is what William James perceived in his pluralist period, but pluralism, or so it seems to me, is itself only a stage in a path that pushes onwards into regions much more difficult to explore. It is foolish to imagine that human thinking can rest contented once it has discovered the category of *severalness*. In a plural universe, the several elements are inevitably converted by thought into a new whole—and the same insoluble problem faces us again. The truth really seems to be that, in this context, we have to free ourselves from all categories that are those of quantity, of the quantifiable. It is the task of the metaphysical imagination, at this point, to go on to a renewal of its fundamental categories.

But perhaps I shall be more easily understood if I express myself as follows: I cannot postulate an absolute totality, a complete and final whole, without putting myself, to some extent surreptitiously, that is, in a disguised fashion, in the place of that whole: but I have clearly recognized my own situation to be a finite one, I have grasped that I am one *among* others, or rather one *with* others. Between myself and others something is built up which transcends any relationship properly so called, a *super-relationship* which it is not in my power to transform into a sort of ideal object, which I might mentally manipulate as one manipulates a formula. But this, which is already entirely true of myself and my neighbours, becomes truer still if by any path at all I can raise myself up to the idea of God, or, more precisely, if I have recognized God's presence. So much for pantheism. As far as manicheism is concerned, the question must be framed in rather different terms. It would certainly not be misleading to remind ourselves that our situation on earth implies the acceptance of what one might call a sort of practical manicheism; by this I mean—and this again perhaps comes home to men more strikingly in our own period than in any other—that in so far as he is a moral being, each one of us has to recognize the irreducible opposition between the good and the evil, each one of us has to opt for the good against the evil. However, this practical manicheism, which has to do with the fashion in which good and evil present themselves to the fighting conscience, could not be transformed without a grave abuse into a theoretical or metaphysical manicheism which would treat good and evil as principles of equal reality disputing for empire over men. When I say that such a transformation would be an illicit operation, I am speaking from a purely philosophical point of view, not from the point of view of a Christian believer conforming to the decision of a Council which, more than fifteen centuries ago, proclaimed the heretical character of the Manichean doctrine; I mean merely that manicheism, in so far as it is a metaphysical doctrine, implies a failure to recognize or to interpret properly the nature of human experience at its heights. The best thing to do here, I think, will be to take a precise example.

It is obvious enough that the doctor who is fighting against disease and death has no need at all to ask questions about their metaphysical essence. He is following his proper vocation if he simply regards them as irreducibly evil, and struggles against them with all the resources at his disposal. But it is none the less obvious that the sick man—and I am thinking particularly of the incurably sick man—can come to consider his illness from a quite other point of view, though this will not prevent him from giving his confidence to the doctor who is striving to cure him. The illness from which he is suffering may appear to him, if not all the time, at least at certain privileged moments, as a pathway and not merely as an obstacle. I should be tempted to say that the philosopher, in the presence of that evil which is not only *before him* but also *within him*, can adopt an attitude analogous to that of the sick man, who, through a real conversion—and I am not taking this word in a specifically religious sense—has managed to make himself in some sense master of his illness, and to reduce it to a subordinate position.

Let us further add that the philosopher will not recognize it as either possible or permissible to treat evil as something which, though in a shadowy and opaque way, is substantial: as something which could be endowed with intrinsic existence. This is not to say that he will agree to minimize evil, in the fashion of Leibniz, for instance, by saying that it is only a least good or an absence of good. In the eyes of the philosopher, evil is a mystery, but that phrase has not the vague sense that some readers might be tempted to suppose. When I say that evil is a mystery, I mean, very precisely, this: in no sense can the notion of evil be assimilated to that of a defect of function which could be remedied by suitable methods. The expression 'radical evil', which both Kant and Schelling used, corresponds to something profoundly real: and that again means that, if I am entirely sincere, I must recognize that evil is not only *before* me, but *within me*, in a sense it is something that rings me round, it lays siege to me. Yet, and in a quite other sense, I am bound to affirm that now and for ever evil is conquered or rather annulled, it is as if it were not, and this is just what manicheism is unwilling to admit.

On what do we base this last affirmation? Is it, or is it not, the expression of some kind of religious faith? But I have already said, on the contrary, that the philosopher, as such, cannot consider himself as the faithful vassal of any sort of church whatsoever. Am I appealing then to the notion of value? Shall we have to assert that there are certain values which the philosopher cannot avoid postulating as absolute? To be sure, this is a vocabulary which, for the last fifty years, has had a predominant place in numerous schools of philosophy. However, for my part, I must confess—and here again I believe I am in accord with the author of *Sein und Zeit*—that it is a vocabulary which is beginning to satisfy me less and less. We do not speak of value until we are in the presence of a preliminary *devaluation*, which draws our attention to the concept; I mean by this that there is in the word 'value' a certain compensating function that makes us use the word rather specially where something real and substantial has been lost. What we call value, to-day, in fact, is what was formerly called the modes or perfections of being. To me personally the kind of philosophy for which 'value' is a key term seems an abortive attempt to recover through our words what we have really lost from our thoughts.

For what we have to do with, really, is a decisive option: the choice between being and not being. To-day, however, we must recognize that it is possible for non-being to be preferred, possible also for it to wear the mask of being, and it is just such masquerades which the philosopher is in duty bound to denounce. It is easy enough to understand that I cannot denounce such a masquerade on the part of non-being without at the same time affirming the transcendence of being, and it is just, of course, this affirmation which implies that, finally and fundamentally, the intrinsic existence or dark substantiality of evil can and must be denied . . . Of the kind of masquerade to which I have just made allusion, I shall put forward here one example only, that of the sort of canonization of history which not only Marxists of the stricter rule but all those more or less hypnotized by Hegelian thought, or at least by the popularized interpretations of that so widely diffused in our own day, are tending towards. Let us see what has happened to-day to that famous and in my opinion infinitely vulnerable formula, *Weltgeschichte ist Weltgericht.* In the most simple-minded fashion one stamps with one's approval certain modes of social existence or organization, and declares that they are in accordance with the general flow of history; while, on the other hand, other modes, a monarchical polity or one dominated by some aristocratic ideal, will be declared retrogressive and opposed to the current of events, as if on the one hand we were really in a position to make affirmations about what is going to happen in the future, and on the other hand—and above all—as if what is going to happen will inevitably, and properly, be the best thing that can happen. Such optimism is obviously a transposition to the key of rather rudimentary thinking of an idea whose origins are mystical, like the idea of the *pleroma* or the *parousia.* But from that genuinely eschatological point of view, what prevents us from believing that at the end of time only a persecuted minority will incarnate in its life and in its thinking the truth of Christ—while what will prevail in the world, in the most ostentatious and tyrannical fashion, will be an apparently triumphant technocracy, but a technocracy destined to collapse and crumble as soon as it is touched by the Spirit?

Let us make ourselves clear here: I do not say that this point of view (which, in so far as I am a believing Christian, I am rather disposed to make my own) ought to or even could be that of the philosopher. But the philosopher is bound to take it into consideration, as a possibility, and a possibility perhaps in accordance with religious faith and its demands, and as such to contrast it with an optimism rooted not in reason but in prejudice.

In this context, it seems necessary to me to clarify as much as possible the stand that the philosopher should take; let me say categorically that he ought not, for instance, to transform himself into a prophet. Yet the notion of prophetic thought is an equivocal one, for the prophet can take *his* stance at a number of very different levels. On the one hand there is the genuine prophet, whose genuineness, to be sure, can hardly ever be recognized except by the Church, or only so in conditions into which I cannot go in detail here; the genuine prophet appears to us as gifted with supernatural powers and called to a supernatural mission. With the genuine prophet, the philosopher cannot help feeling in sympathy, but at the same time this sympathy, one should emphasize, is always of an anguished sort, for the very reason that prophecy is always like lightning, flashing transversely across the hard and twisty paths along which the philosopher must grope his way. This prophetic foreshortening frightens the philosopher just because of the infinite danger of distortion it implies; yet this infinite danger has also something positive and one might say necessary about it . . . Yet there is also the false prophet, who remains at the level of experience, who bases his prophecies on some science such as biology, economics, sociology. Obviously, such a false prophet may be sincere; yet it is, I think, the duty of the philosopher not to weary in denouncing the illegitimacy of his claims. Such denunciations, of course, ought not to take the form of invective. A philosophy worthy of the name ought to be incapable of descending to the level of the pamphleteer; philosophy should certainly always retain the critical spirit, but any kind of criticism worth calling criticism implies an anxiety to be fair that is profoundly foreign to the pamphleteering spirit. Philosophical activity also presupposes a certain native courage in the philosopher—for the philosophical spirit is bound to see itself slandered, both by the fanatic and by the false prophet, who in the long run always runs the risk of himself becoming fanaticized.

It follows from all this that the situation of the philosopher as he confronts our contemporary world is almost the most risky and exposed situation one can imagine. I do not merely mean that the philosopher may expect to pay for his rashness in the depths of some Soviet, or other, prison. The danger is also, and perhaps above all, an inner one. It is very hard for the philosopher to-day to resist the temptation to flee, I will not say into the realm of science—for science, where it is truthfully pursued, retains even to-day all its value, all its dignity—but into the realm of some pretended science, such as psychoanalysis for example, a realm where science bursts its bonds and claims to have grasped the keys of spiritual reality. But that is not the only danger: yielding to what a contemporary thinker calls 'the nostalgia for being', the philosopher may deviate into mysticism: this is what I would call the higher escapism, but it is escapism all the same. On this topic I am not sure that I have expressed myself clearly enough in former books of mine, and perhaps in fact this is a temptation to which I have occasionally yielded myself. While gladly recognizing that mysticism can, to all appearances, reach places that are impenetrable to philosophy, the philosopher nevertheless owes it to himself, I think, to maintain, though without undue display of emotion, the necessity of that way of thought, and I would even say of that way of existence, which are his own. For it may be that this specific way of thought and existence is closely linked to the safeguarding of what has traditionally been denoted by the now rather discredited term, 'civilization'. I have a deep conviction, at least, that the fate of philosophy and that of civilization are directly and intimately linked. Perhaps one might say that between the world of techniques and that of pure spirituality, the mediation of the philosopher is becoming more and more indispensable. Otherwise, there is a danger of the technician's attitude infringing on a domain that ought to remain inviolate: but, on the other hand, through a natural but dangerous reaction, there is a risk of those who pursue the purely spiritual life passing a verdict of condemnation on all techniques, a verdict that perhaps will not and cannot be put into practical effect, but that might, nevertheless, plunge many minds into a state of terrible confusion. There, no doubt, lies the greatest evil of our time. I have said, in the first volume of my Gifford Lectures, *The Mystery of Being*, that we are living in a world which seems to be founded on the refusal to reflect. It is the place of the philosopher, and perhaps his place only, to attack this contemporary confusion, not in a presumptuous way certainly, not with any illusions about what the effect of his attack is likely to be, but with the feeling that here lies a duty which cannot be evaded, a duty from which he cannot withdraw himself without betraying his true mission.

CHAPTER II

THE FANATICIZED CONSCIOUSNESS

THE reasons why I have chosen to speak here of fanaticism are too obvious to be worth going into in detail: fanaticism literally rings us round. I am not thinking only of Stalinist fanaticism. The anti-Stalinist Communists, particularly the Titoists, are without any doubt fanatics also. But that is not the whole story; the Nazism which, according to the most competent observers, is perhaps being revived in Germany and Austria is also a fanaticism: the worst of all of them. And if one is perfectly frank, one must admit that even religions which are genuine in their principles can, if I may put it so, become fanaticized, just as an originally healthy organic tissue can become cancerous.

Why speak, however, of 'the fanaticized consciousness' and not simply of 'fanaticism'? Because, I reply, words in 'ism' often represent an illicit process of thinking which we should avoid as much as possible. What demands all our attention is a certain mode of being of human consciousness or awareness, or rather a mode of existence of that consciousness. To-day we can in fact see very clearly that until our own period this notion of consciousness has been always very inadequately explained and even conceived. I am thinking of Kant particularly, and of part of his philosophical posterity, not the Hegelian school, but rather the neo-critical school in France and Germany. These believed that it was possible to reduce consciousness or awareness in general to an act of becoming aware, of grasping through one's awareness—an act which did not lend itself to any further description and which, in consequence, could not be conceived as changing or deteriorating in any way, Thus an impossibly wide gap tended to open out between what one might call this transcendental philosophy and concrete experience, more particularly psycho-pathological experience—but the latter must have its roots in the structure of so-called 'normal' experience. It is, in fact, only in our own day that medical observation has led people to speak of a 'diseased' consciousness. But one should add that the deepest philosophical research, perhaps already in Husserl's work, but certainly in the work of his successors, had reached conclusions that tended to converge with those of medical psychologists. I do not want to insist on this point; but as I am going to try to make a succinct phenomenological analysis of the fanaticized consciousness, I am bound to explain here just what, from a point of view which is far from being exclusively my own, we must understand by a phenomenological analysis.

I would remind the reader that Husserl, following Brentano, and developing also certain philosophical ideas of the Middle Ages, finally clarified the 'intentional' character of consciousness. That phrase means that our consciousness is essentially a consciousness *of*, or more precisely a consciousness *directed towards*, something. It is directed towards a reality from which it cannot be severed except by a process of vicious abstraction. I shall have to show, therefore, just what change for the worse is expressed in the 'intentional' direction of a fanaticized consciousness. What is important is to grasp the fact that this change for the worse is not wholly and exclusively subjective; it has not to do with what properly speaking can be called a state of consciousness, but rather with the way in which consciousness directs itself to something other than itself, and this object of consciousness cannot be neglected as it was by the psychologists of the past who, in fact, considered only *states of consciousness*.

After carrying out this, of course, merely schematic analysis, it will be my purpose to seek out the reasons why this malady of fanaticism is becoming almost epidemic, and I shall try very summarily to show what remedies are available, particularly in the field of education. It will be impossible, however, to avoid trespassing on the domains of metaphysics and religion, and I must excuse myself in advance in case I find that, in spite of my dislike of doing so, I have to shock and horrify minds whose natural bent is towards dogmatism. I should add at once, however, that there can be no question of expounding and exploiting this problem in a sense favourable to scepticism. For scepticism is, just as much as dogmatism, in contradiction to those structural conditions that make consciousness possible. It is more than doubtful whether a sceptical attitude can confer the least immunity from fanaticism on the man who favours it, and it is even to be feared that, by a sort of dialectical process, it leads in the long run to fanaticism.

The first obvious observation to be made is that the fanatic never sees himself *as* a fanatic; it is only the non-fanatic who can recognize him as a fanatic; so that when this judgment, or this accusation, is made, the fanatic can always say that he is misunderstood and slandered.

To be sure, this observation may awaken a certain uneasiness in the mind of a sincere thinker, who is attempting to concentrate his attention on the fanaticized consciousness; he may be inclined to ask himself whether, in accusing somebody of being a fanatic, he is not himself, as a non-fanatic, yielding to a purely subjective and emotional reaction. Perhaps it is not possible to dismiss this objection out of hand; it is only after our analysis has been worked out in some detail that we shall be able to dismiss it.

What are the combined conditions that must be fulfilled if we are to be in a position to say of some man or other, 'He is a fanatic'? Or, in more precise language, what is the fanaticizing power, and where does its stronghold lie? One might be inclined, as a first guess, to say that *ideas* as such have the power of making men fanatical; and certainly this is not absolutely off the mark, but it is not the whole truth, either. First of all, it is not every idea that can make men fanatical; it is not enough even for an idea to acquire an obsessive character, an obsessive grip. Think, for instance, of Balthazar Claes in Balzac's *The Quest of the Absolute*, who is obsessed and perhaps crazily so, but is certainly not a fanatic. We might be tempted to say, without any further reflection, that fanaticism is essentially religious; but that again seems to me at once true and false; true from the point of view of a merely objective description of religion, but more deeply false, since at this level all objective description inevitably and essentially distorts the reality to which it is applied, or more precisely because objective description tends to exclude and to make void of significance the distinction between a true religion and a false one. We have to recognize that a true religion cannot have this power of making men fanatical and that, on the contrary, wherever this fanaticizing power does exist, there is a perversion of religion.

But what, then, has enabled us to say that from the point of view of objective description fanaticism is of the order of religious activity or experience? It is the fact that the fanatic cannot be an isolated being, that on the contrary he exists *among* others, and that between these others and himself there is formed what one would be tempted to call a kind of agglutination, though I would rather speak of a unity or identity of harmonic range. This unity—or this identity—is felt as a link which exalts, and the fanaticism of one man is always kept alight by contact with the fanaticism of another. Also, one could say that fanaticism is always centred upon an over-developed consciousness of 'ourselves, the others' as a group.

But it is not enough to say this. It also seems that at least in the immense majority of cases fanaticism will not be centred on an idea as such, an idea considered in its abstract scope and implication, but upon an individual who is the embodiment and source of the idea or, like a vector in mathematics, determines its position in relation to other ideas: who, in a word, focusses the idea for the group. The disappearance of this individual who acts as a central focal area will always bring with it the danger of a serious crisis for the fanaticized mind. However, one ought here to distinguish different types of cases. If this focal individual disappears simply because of an illness or an accident, he may survive himself as a sort of deified presiding ghost. This is even more true if he is assassinated. Murder is sufficient in itself to unleash the desire for vengeance, and that desire cannot fail to have an exacerbating effect on fanaticism itself. Nevertheless, it is still necessary that a kind of substitution should take place, that the dead man should have a successor who may act as his *locum tenens*. If this substitution does not take place, the group tends to drift apart, to lose its cohesion, and this, at least in the long run, is dangerous to fanaticism. A very different case is that in which the focal individual in some manner betrays the idea of which he is supposed to be the living incarnation. The resulting failure of cohesion in the group can be much more serious in this case, since we are at the level of actual existence, and since the individual is not thought of as representing in a merely contingent fashion an entity which transcends him. The link between individual and idea is much more immediate, more concrete. Therefore, from the point of view of actual existence if not of abstract logic, such a betrayal of an idea by the individual who represents it runs the risk of reacting on the idea itself—precisely because it is not the idea as such, as we have already noticed, that has properly speaking the power of creating fanaticism. Let us observe, moreover, that any sort of failure of cohesion, any disorder in the ranks of the group, endangers fanaticism, because fanaticism excludes such driftings apart in principle. This failure of cohesion can present itself as the weakening of some thin surface which has been stretched too far; but such a weakening can always become a rending or a collapse.

This, no doubt, is where we ought to bring in the notion of the masses. Just by looking around us we are in a position to say that the masses, *qua* masses, are essentially the stuff of which fanaticism is made. It is relevant here to refer to the thoughts on this subject put forward by Ortega y Gasset in his book, *The Revolt of the Masses*. This Spanish writer calls our attention to the fact that in groups whose character is precisely that of *not* being crowds or masses, the way the feelings and emotions of their members come together is by centring on some desire, some idea or ideal, which in itself excludes the adherence of very great numbers to the group. The mass may, on the contrary, be defined, in so far as it is a psychological datum, as existing at a level below that at which individuals deliberately organize themselves into groups. A given individual belongs to the mass not only when his estimation of himself, good or bad, does not rest on his rightly judging that he has some kind of special qualification, but also when, feeling himself just the same sort of person as everybody else, he does not experience any anxiety because of this feeling but finds it rather reassuring, on the contrary, to feel that he is just as others are. 'The characteristic of this world we are living in to-day is that the mediocre soul, knowing itself to be mediocre, has the boldness to assert the rights of mediocrity, and to impose them everywhere . . . The mass makes a *tabula rasa* of everything that is not like itself, of everything that is excellent, individual, specially qualified, choice. Whoever is not like everybody else, whoever does not think like everybody else, runs the risk of being eliminated. And it is obvious that this "everybody else" is not the "everybody else" of former days. In the old days, when we talked about "everybody" we normally meant the masses and the dissident specialized minorities considered as one complete group. But to-day "everybody" means the masses, and the masses only'. These words of Ortega's are, it seems to me, one of the most lucid diagnoses that have been made of the sickness of our contemporary world. And since the already distant date at which his book was composed, the situation has been getting worse, and worse even from a point of view like Ortega's own. For he wrote at a time before it was clear how accessible the masses are to propaganda and how easily turned into fanatics. 'It is not a matter of saying', he wrote a little farther on, 'that the mass-man is a fool. On the contrary, he is more awake and alert than ever in the past, he has even a considerable intellectual capacity, but his gifts are no use to him. . . . Once and for all, it must be said that he is perfectly satisfied with the accumulation of commonplace ideas, of prejudices, of shreds and scraps of other men's notions, or of mere words empty of meaning, which chance has flung pell-mell to mix up in his head.' There is a complete agreement between this portrait of the mass-man and that of the French *On*, the German *Man*, the English *People* or *They* (as in '*They* say', or '*People* think') as defined by Heidegger in his great work.

But we ought to be able to see more clearly just for what reason the mass-man is so easily turned into a fanatic. What I seem to myself to have grasped is this, that such permeability is due to the fact that man, that the individual, in order to belong to the mass, to be a mass-man, has had, as a preliminary, though without having had the least awareness of it, to divest himself of that substantial reality which was linked to his initial individuality or rather to the fact of his belonging to a small actual group. The incredibly sinister role of the press, the cinema, the radio, has consisted in passing that original reality through a pair of flattening rollers to substitute for it a superimposed pattern of ideas and images with no real roots in the deep being of the subject of this experiment. But does it not seem just as if propaganda offered a kind of nourishment to the unconscious hunger felt by beings thus deprived of their own proper reality? Propaganda will thus create a kind of second and entirely factitious nature, but a nature which can only be sustained and kept alive by a passion, by, in fact, precisely the passion of fanaticism. We ought certainly to add here that the basis of this passion is fear, that it implies an unconfessed emotional insecurity that converts itself into an outward aggressiveness. It is by the existence of this secret fear that we can most conveniently explain the refusal, involved in all types of fanaticism, to bring basic assumptions into question; and we shall have to ask ourselves in what the essential nature of this refusal lies. Such an examination of the nature of the fanatic's refusal to discuss his presuppositions is all the more necessary as we are here in a rather badly charted territory, where there is a risk of confusion arising in our minds between fanaticism and faith.

Certainly, it is clear enough that it is the duty of the religious believer to treat the doubts that may sometimes assail him as temptations; but it is essential that we should ask ourselves under what conditions this is permissible.

We must see that this desire not to reopen discussion is justifiable only if it is linked to the complete and final transcendence of the object of faith, a transcendence which itself confers on the desire its only valid basis. In fact, this complete and final, this absolute transcendence is only another aspect of what has traditionally been called the infinite: that infinite which, by its very notion, surpasses in every way our powers of comprehension and before which we can only acknowledge our nothingness. But in so far as we do really recognize this infinite or transcendent reality of God, we rigorously interdict ourselves from reopening discussion on what we have thus affirmed; for such a reopening of discussion would imply a claim on our parts which, by acknowledging God's reality, we had already abdicated for once and all.

But it is obvious also that if, for this infinite God, we substitute an idol of any sort whatsoever, this reopening of the discussion ceases to be blameworthy. It becomes, on the contrary, a duty imposed on us by our honesty as thinking beings. For it is of the very nature of an idol that it can be broken or merely that it can incite a spirit of revolt in the man who at first revered it.

It is important to note here that I am not speaking from a narrowly Christian perspective. This transcendent and infinite God I am speaking of is also the God of Islam and the Jews. But if fanaticism can creep back into such religions—as we are well aware that it has done among the followers of Mahomet, though no more strikingly so than among certain Jews and among very many Christians—that is, it seems to me, only due to the growth and intervention between man and God of certain mediating powers, such as the Church or the Prophet, which, instead of remaining mere mediators, are endowed by the fanaticized consciousness with certain prerogatives quite incompatible with the weakness proper to the creature *qua* creature.

The key idea that we have to keep hold of does seem to me, after all, a very simple one, and nothing would be easier than to illustrate it with the aid of contemporary examples: the Marx of *Das Kapital* as he is viewed by Communist fanatics to-day or the Hitler of *Mein Kampf* as he was viewed by the Nazis. To put these two cases on one level may shock some of my readers but it is, in this context, unavoidable. In both cases, a book is treated as a holy book, though it is the work of a human creature whose infallibility we have no reason to believe in. In such cases, the decision not to reopen discussion is fanatical in its essence, and this decision is at the root of all the calamities fanaticism draws in its train. The day for instance on which the average Marxist would be willing to recognize that the works of Marx arose from a special historical context, since profoundly modified, and therefore have not a validity that transcends time, would mark the end of Communist fanaticism. In fact, the greatest merit of the critical spirit is that it tends to cure fanaticism, and it is logical enough that in our own fanatical times the critical spirit should tend to disappear, should no longer even be paid lip-service as a value. However, we ought to try to disentangle the reasons why, in the last quarter of a century, the critical spirit has declined to such a frightening extent. There can be no doubt that an untrue and deplorable vitalist philosophy, of which some seeds are to be found in Nietzsche, others in Sorel, and so on, has, at the surface level of ideas, fostered this decline; but, if we probe more deeply, as we ought to, we can see that this vitalism has managed to get a grip of men's minds only because of a previous evolution of their thinking and feeling at a deeper level. It would be relevant, I think, here to point out the sinister part played by speed, by belief in speed as a value, by, in a word, a kind of impatience that has had a profound effect in changing even the very rhythms of the life of the spirit for the worse.

On the other hand, we ought to ask ourselves under just what conditions an idea or a person, or more precisely the dangerous complex constituted by idea *and* person, tends to acquire this power of engendering fanaticism. I shall take care not to make excessively general assertions of the sort that smack of a kind of historicist philosophy, which is itself an extremely risky mode of thought. Let us be content to describe what we see around us. One simple fact should be obvious to the most superficial observer: it is that very many young men who have received an intensive intellectual training, and whose whole background, it would seem, ought to encourage the growth of the critical spirit, tend to engulf themselves on the contrary in a fanaticism which radically isolates them from those who do not think as they do. No doubt it is wise in principle to refuse to question the sincerity of such young men. It would be far too easy a way out simply to claim that they are nothing more than ambitious opportunists. What we are in the presence of is, rather, a pathological state, but we are not sure whether it is the reasoning mind or the affective sensibility that is ill; rather it may be the case that the illness arises where reason and sensibility try to adapt themselves to each other.

There is, it seems to me, one aspect of fanaticism which we have not yet sufficiently underlined. The fanaticized consciousness remains, as it were, numb and unresponsive to everything to which its own compass needle does not respond. When you speak to a Stalinist about the millions of wretches who have been deported to the shores of the White Sea or to other distant regions where they are condemned after a more or less brief interval to die of hunger or cold, if the man you are talking to does not merely flatly deny that this is true, he will probably say to you that this is one of the harsh necessities of a period of transition. The shocking proverb, 'You cannot make an omelette without breaking eggs', is the expression of this argument at a trivial level. But our Stalinist could not make this answer unless he had put himself into a state of mind in which he was utterly unable to represent to himself the real nature of the facts under discussion; insensibility is here allied to an almost total deficiency of imagination: or rather these are two aspects of one and the same phenomenon. This phenomenon can very properly be called pathological, because it is of the same order as that observed by a doctor whose patient fails to react to certain stimuli. To be sure, it is of the very nature of language that it allows itself to be interpreted in all sorts of ways; and it might be claimed that what we have here is not something pathological but rather the expression of a noble and joyous *amor fati*. But this is like claiming that the feverish excitement of certain consumptives indicates an expansion of vitality. The very possibility of such a claim being made shows that our contemporary world is falling prey to a confusion, the like of which has not been seen since the ages of barbarism: a confusion not only between the categories of good and evil but between what we must call life and death.

From this point of view, we should be getting to closer grips with our problem, if we asked ourselves what are some of the factors of this state of partial insensibility, which seems to have the same paralysing effect on the mind as tetanus on the body; it is, in fact, very probably not in psychology, understood in the current sense of the word, but in a kind of biology of the mind that we ought to seek for our explanations. I am thinking particularly of the phenomenon of fatigue. It is as hard to make one's own fatigue the object of intellectual attention as to make one's own pain such an object; and one can even doubt whether the experience of fatigue is really translatable into conceptual terms.

Seeking to avoid any rash generalizations, I think we can nevertheless say this about our contemporary world. There are to-day an increasing number of people whose awareness is, in the strict sense of the phrase, without a focus; and the techniques which have transformed the framework of daily life for such people at such a prodigious pace—I am thinking particularly of the cinema and the radio—are making a most powerful contribution towards this defocalizing process. What I mean is this. One may, it seems to me, lay it down as a principle that the human creature under normal conditions finds his bearings in relation to other people, and also to physical objects, that are not only close to him in space but linked to him by a feeling of intimacy. Of this feeling of intimacy, I would say that in itself it tends to create a focus for human awareness. One might go farther and speak of a kind of constellation, at once material and spiritual, which under normal conditions assembles itself around each human being. But, for a great many reasons which it would be superfluous to enumerate, this kind of constellation round the individual life is, in a great many countries, in process of dissolution. This is true above all, of course, for the proletariat of the great cities, but there are also a great many intellectuals (who deceive themselves seriously when they believe that they can become the conscience of the proletariat and reflect its aspirations) in whose cases this dissolution happens in a very different way.

However, for this real focus of human awareness, which, even if it has not been wholly destroyed, has at least almost wholly lost its power of spreading warmth and light around it, various kinds of imaginary foci do tend to substitute themselves. And though this phenomenon of substitution is a mysterious one, I think its causes lie deep in human nature. The imaginary focus can be situated in space or time, or rather in space and time at once—in a mythical space and time: in the idyllic Russia of the readers of *Humanité* or *The Daily Worker*, or in the classless society which will be established by the proletarian revolution. But the false millenarianism of the Hitlerian doctrinaries also implied an imaginary focus of this sort; and one is forced to add that every kind of fanaticism, even the strictly religious kind, seems to build itself up around a centre of this sort, whether that centre is called Mecca or Rome. Perhaps Rudolf Kassner was trying to express something of this sort in his book on the nineteenth century when he said that in fanaticism there was a sort of permutation of roles between the understanding and the imagination; the imagination takes over the understanding's function. But what I do seem to glimpse, more certainly, is this: the relation thus created between consciousness and its imaginary focus is, to recur to the image I used a short time ago, numbing and paralysing to consciousness itself—like tetanus to the body. It is not enough to say that this relation has its basis in an unwarranted claim or an act of defiance, that it implies, 'I affirm this, *I* do, whatever anyone else says'. It also implies a wish to *wipe out* anyone who dares to denounce the claim as false. We could express this neatly by talking of an affirmation as *charged* with fanaticism, precisely as if it were physically charged with a dangerous electric current. Of course, there is something hard to conceive, something that even resists conceptual expression, in all this: as in the case, which we were dealing with a short time ago, of fatigue. We might say that the fanatic transfers to the level of thought, or to what would be that level if it could, processes which are strictly of the body: it is, I suppose, precisely in so far as it becomes corporealized in this way that thought *is* fanatical. But we ought to notice the great gap between this notion of the corporealization of thought and that of thought becoming properly incarnate; of incarnation in the true sense, this attempt to express, *as* thought, irrational and violent bodily impulses, is only an aberration and perversion.

But it thus becomes very easy to recognize where the difference between faith and fanaticism lies.

Fanaticism is essentially *opinion;* opinion pushed to paroxysm; with everything that the notion of opinion may imply of blinded ignorance as to its own nature. Let us notice also that, whatever ends the fanatic is aiming at or thinks he is aiming at, even if he wishes to gather men together, he can only in fact separate them; but as his own interests cannot lie in effecting this separation, he is led, as we have seen, to wish to wipe his opponents out. And when he is thinking of these opponents, he takes care to form the most degrading images of them possible—they are 'lubricious vipers' or 'hyenas and jackals with typewriters'—and the ones that reduce them to most grossly material terms. In fact, he no longer thinks of these opponents except as material obstacles to be overturned or smashed down. Having abandoned the behaviour of a thinking being, he has lost even the feeblest notion of what a thinking being, outside himself, could be. It is understandable therefore that he should make every effort to deny in advance the rights and qualifications of those whom he wishes to eliminate; and that he should regard all means to this end as fair. We are back here again at the techniques of degradation. It cannot be asserted too strongly or repeated too often that those the Nazis made use of in their camps—techniques for degrading their victims in their own eyes, for making mud and filth of them—and those which Soviet propagandists use to discredit their adversaries, are not essentially different though we should, in fairness, add that sadism, properly so called, is not to be found in the Russian camps. And it is not enough to say even this. We must add that the Soviet propagandists seek to foster in the adversary, through physical and psychological processes not yet known to us in complete detail, a spirit of complicity which will make him prepare and assure his own ruin.

What does seem to me essential is that we should grasp the terrible logic, the logic of death, at work here. Such manifestations are not, though we tend to think so, mere monstrous aberrations. They are nothing but the logical corollaries of fanaticism; they are not a phenomenon, foreign to fanaticism, which has somehow or other been superimposed on it. They derive from the fact that fanaticism is, of its very nature, incompatible with any regard for truth; and as truth itself is not really separable from our regard for it, we need not hesitate to say that the fanatic is the enemy of truth: even if only because he seeks to monopolize truth for his own profit. And this is so at all levels.

But what should have become almost blindingly clear to us over the last few years is that the fates of truth and justice are linked in such a way that it becomes impossible even to distinguish one fate from the other. As the greatest thinkers in the history of mankind have at all times seen—and I am thinking particularly not only of Plato, but also of Spinoza—there can be no justice where there is no respect for truth. Only, when we talk of having a 'respect for truth', we do not mean merely that we are going to use high-sounding phrases; we mean that we are going to keep all the channels open, sometimes exceedingly tenuous channels, by which we can hope, I will not say to attain truth, but at least to approach truth.

Here we also see why, as I said at the beginning of this chapter, the sceptical attitude is of no practical use here. It is in the name of truth, and of the structural conditions that make truth a possibility, that fanaticism must be fought; and not in the name of some sort of pliable relativism according to which all opinions, after all, are worth something, and yet remain equally below the level of an inaccessible reality. One might even ask whether, in its actual effect if not in its essential nature, the sceptical attitude does not prepare the ground on which fanaticism will later be able to work with greater facility.

I would further observe that in France recently we have lived and we are still living in an atmosphere of latent fanaticism, with intermittent outbreaks, and it was because I was aware of this that in the first few months after the Liberation I wrote the study published in Canada under the title, *The Philosophy of the Purge: A Contribution to a Theory of Hypocrisy at the Level of Politics.* Will it be objected that, where there is hypocrisy, there cannot be fanaticism? We should note carefully that we have to do here with a single process of degradation. Insincerity or bad faith, which is inseparable from fanaticism, can be, in a very imperfect way, aware of itself; and then it gives the observer the impression of hypocrisy. Such insincerity or bad faith exists almost everywhere to-day. It is particularly in evidence in men's approaches to certain current problems that seem almost insoluble, like that of Indo-China: I have said elsewhere that such problems not only swarm to-day but have acquired a virulence that was perhaps unknown in the past. They help to create an atmosphere very favourable to fanaticism. It is given only to a tiny chosen few to recognize the inextricable as such; from the practical point of view, the inextricable looks like a blind alley. In such case, the urge of the fanatic becomes something like the urge to operate, to have recourse to the knife, when an illness has been dragging on for years, to make an end of it, one way or another. In both situations, the results of such a course are generally disastrous.

CHAPTER III

THE SPIRIT OF ABSTRACTION, AS A FACTOR MAKING FOR WAR

TO-DAY there does exist an indissoluble connection between lying and war: *to-day*, I emphasize, for we are not asserting that there is some necessary and logical connection between the mere notions of lying and making war. But in the actual world we are living in it is impossible not to recognize that making war is linked to lying, and to lying in a double form: lying to others and lying to oneself; and these two forms themselves, for that matter, are very closely linked and perhaps not even ideally separable from each other.

A person who is not lying to himself can hardly fail to observe that in its modern forms war is a disaster from which no counterbalancing advantage can be reaped, except perhaps in the case of a purely aggressive war directed against an unarmed adversary; and even there no doubt the advantage is only an apparent one. However, in the case of such an act of aggression, war has ceased properly speaking to be war, and has degenerated into mere organized banditry, though people will no doubt attempt to camouflage this banditry by describing the aggression as 'a punitive expedition'; the inexhaustible resources of propaganda will then be put to work to help this camouflage.

In every other sort of case, that is to say wherever there is a conflict between two adversaries who are really armed, we know to-day that the risks of every kind are unimaginable, and that the general destruction to all appearances transcends any advantage which anyone might hope to derive from it. The facts are there, so plain that he who runs may read, and it is difficult to conceive how the lesson they teach could still remain a dead letter, if not to the mass of men, at least to the so-called responsible people on whom the fate of the mass of men depends. But it is obvious even before we have begun to reflect on this situation that lying, here, is a determinant factor. It is only through organized lying that we can hope to make war acceptable to those who must wage or suffer it (we should note in passing that, for practical purposes, the distinction between waging and suffering war, between playing an active and a passive part in war, is vanishing, and this is a point on which we cannot concentrate our attention too closely). In fact, to make war acceptable to-day, hardly anybody would dare to use arguments of mere expediency. The arguments in favour are those of a pseudo-religious necessity or obligation. This category of the 'pseudo-religious' covers racial wars as well as revolutionary and class wars. It would obviously be very easy to show that all propaganda with this sort of aim has its basis in lying.

But all this is by way of preliminary. The investigation which I am seeking to outline here takes its rise in my concern to determine what is the exact relation between lying and abstraction. Here again we should notice that we are not seeking to establish a conceptual relationship between these two notions, but only to work out their actual relations at this period of human history.

It would be convenient here to distinguish between the notion of abstraction as such, and that of the spirit of abstraction, but it is not very easy to establish this distinction firmly. Abstraction, as such, is a mental operation to which we must have recourse if we are seeking to achieve a determinate purpose of any sort. Psychologists have demonstrated with perfect clarity the close internal link between abstraction and action. To abstract, in a word, is to make a preliminary clearing of the ground, and of course this clearing of the ground can appear the strictly reasonable thing to do. This means that the human mind must retain a precise and distinct awareness of those methodical omissions which are necessary if an envisaged result is to be obtained. But it can happen that the mind, yielding to a sort of fascination, ceases to be aware of these prior conditions that justify abstraction and deceives itself about the nature of what is, in itself, nothing more than a method, one might almost say nothing more than an expedient. The spirit of abstraction is not separable from this contempt for the concrete conditions of abstract thinking, I would even say that it *is* this contempt. Perhaps it would not be misleading to say that the spirit of abstraction can in certain respects be regarded as a transposition of the attitudes of imperialism to the mental plane. Possibly Baron Seillière, that little-read philosopher, has seen this as clearly as anyone. As soon as we accord to any category, isolated from all other categories, an arbitrary primacy, we are victims of the spirit of abstraction. But what matters also is to see clearly that, in spite of appearances to the contrary, this operation, of arbitrarily isolating a category, is not really essentially an intellectual one. It would be useful to have recourse here to a kind of generalized psychoanalysis that would throw light on the invariably passional character of the operation in question. This is very strikingly true, for instance, of the victim of the spirit of abstraction who claims to interpret the whole pattern of human reality on the basis of economic facts. To lose one's last illusions on the matter, it is sufficient, for instance, to have heard a Marxist discuss the problems of art. There cannot be a rational justification of any sort for the act by which one claims to subordinate the characteristics of artistic creation, at a given epoch, to the prevailing economic conditions of that epoch. And it is quite certain that in this connection we ought to refer ourselves to the exhaustive analyses of Nietzsche and, more especially, of Scheler, which throw so much light on the part played by resentment in such reductive operations. We should have at this point to make a direct attack on general formulations of the type, '*This* is only *that* . . . *This* is nothing other than *that* . . .', and so on: every depreciatory reduction of this sort has its basis in resentment, that is to say, in passion, and at bottom it corresponds to a violent attack directed against a sort of integrity of the real, an integrity to which only a resolutely concrete mode of thinking can hope to do justice. But what we should also notice is that this depreciatory reduction implies on the other side of the medal a factitious exaltation of the residual element which the victim of the spirit of abstraction is claiming to preserve in its purity, having sacrificed to it what have been defined as mere appearances or mere superstructures. This is a quite general phenomenon and one which stands out, for instance, just as strikingly in the verbal battles of the Surrealists as in Marxist denunciations. And a traditionalist and reactionary philosophy may, of course, lay itself open to similar remarks in so far as it is governed by a spirit of exclusion. However, there is an important distinction to be made here, for such a philosophy does after all imply an attitude of reverence towards the past and towards tradition as a kind of storehouse of divine and human wisdom; all one can say is that this mode of thought, like all others, if it comes under the empire of that spirit of abstraction which rots everything it touches, does run the risk of becoming hard, dry, sterile.

But as soon, of course, as one has become aware of these passions that underly the spirit of abstraction, it becomes possible to understand that they have their place even among the most dangerous of the causes of war. There are a number of urgently relevant observations that force themselves on us here. The most important of them seems to me to be the following: as soon as people (*people*, that is to say, the State or a political party or a faction or a religious sect, or what it may be) claim of me that I commit myself to a warlike action against other human beings whom I must, as a consequence of my commitment, be ready to destroy, it is very necessary from the point of view of those who are influencing me that I lose all awareness of the individual reality of the being whom I may be led to destroy. In order to transform him into a mere impersonal target, it is absolutely necessary to convert him into an abstraction: *the* Communist, *the* anti-Fascist, *the* Fascist, and so on . . . I am not, of course, in any sense making the claim that this is a method which any human mind sets out coldly and consciously to apply. The truth lies much deeper. The fact rather is, or so it seems to me, that the element of resentment in human nature is profoundly linked to a tendency to conceptual dissociation—in this, lying at the opposite pole to the element of admiration.

The latter, in its roots and its innocence, seems to imply rather a kind of tension between the whole of the person who contemplates and the whole of the contemplated person. Let me note in passing—and this does seem to me an observation of the very greatest importance—that the extraordinary setbacks which the contemplative spirit has suffered in our time do seem to be linked on the one hand to the development of the spirit of abstraction and on the other hand, which is a much more serious matter, to the intensification of the warlike spirit in our world. The problem of contemplation and the problem of peace are not merely of one substance with each other, they are really one and the same problem; but once again the point we must emphasize is precisely this, that there cannot fail to be an opposition between the contemplative spirit and a disposition to remain satisfied with abstraction as such.

We ought, I think, to go farther and to observe that our world—and this perhaps is one of the aspects under which it appears most clearly as a world under condemnation—is a world where abstractions become embodied without ceasing to be abstractions: or in other words, they materialize themselves without really becoming incarnate. (As an example that may make my drift clearer, I would observe that the extraordinary poverty and bareness of architecture in the contemporary world is to all appearances linked to this general state of affairs.) It is from this point of view that we ought to consider the sinister use that has been made of the idea of 'the masses' in the modern world. 'The masses'—this seems to me the most typical, the most significant example of an abstraction which remains an abstraction even after it has become real: has become real, I mean, in the pragmatic sense of becoming a force, a power. Such realized abstractions are in some sense pre-ordained for the purposes of war: that is to say, quite simply, for the purposes of human inter-destructiveness. And at this point, indeed, in our argument we might bring in the most various and concrete examples; we might show, for instance, that the great popular papers, with all their evil effects, are linked precisely to this type of abstraction. Taking up again one of the most important themes of my recent researches, I would say that the popular press has by its nature a bias against reflection, against reflection of every type, but also—as a sort of converse of these propositions—that all reflection worthy of the name, that is to say, all reflection conscious of the urgent inner need which is its most secret spring of action, must be exercised for the sake of the concrete, on behalf of the concrete.

These expressions, 'for the sake of the concrete, on behalf of the concrete' have about them a flavour that may surprise the unreflective mind: one might in fact be tempted to suppose that the concrete is what is given at first, is what our thinking must start from. But nothing could be more false than such a supposition: and here Bergson is at one with Hegel. What is given us to start with is a sort of unnamed and unnamable confusion where abstractions, not yet elaborated, are like so many little still unseparated clots of matter. It is only by going through and beyond the process of scientific abstraction that the concrete can be regrasped and reconquered. The problem of peace can be stated in somewhat analogous terms. There is no more dangerous illusion than that of supposing peace to be a kind of preliminary, given state; what is given is something which is not even war, but which contains war in a latent condition. Let us note also that our investigation should here turn towards our own inner states, and that it is by the aid of such a turning of our reflections inward that we can clarify what I said earlier about the relationship between peace and contemplation. We should ask ourselves under what conditions each of us can succeed in being at peace with himself; we know very well that this state of peace is not and cannot be a given condition, a preliminary state, but only a terminus, the most difficult of the states to which we can raise ourselves, the supreme elevation. But we know also that, though certain blinded thinkers have supposed the contrary, I cannot be at peace with myself if I am not at peace with my brothers. I say 'my brothers', and in its final development an investigation of the sort which I have been outlining in this extremely schematic way would have to deal with the notion of fraternity.

But it is, of course, precisely the case that there is not and cannot be any sense of brotherhood in abstraction. In this connection, indeed, nothing could be more deceptive and more full of lies than the formulations with which the great men of the French Revolution allowed themselves to be satisfied. They believed in a simple-minded way, because they found their inspiration in what was all in all an utterly rudimentary philosophy, that liberty, equality, and fraternity could all be placed on the same level. But in my own opinion nothing could be more inaccurate than their thinking here. I hope we shall be able to recognize that equality has to do with the abstract; that it is not men who are equal, for men are not triangles or quadrilaterals. What are equal, what must be postulated as equal, are not human beings but rights and duties which men must reciprocally recognize; for if that recognition is lacking, we have chaos, we have tyranny with all its frightful consequences—the primacy of the most vile over the most noble.

But we become guilty of a tragic error when, from what has to do with rights, we claim to pass to what has to do with men themselves, and it would be easy to show by what sort of dialectic process egalitarianism, properly so called, leads to the monstrous aberrations of which we are the witnesses to-day. This dialectic process is linked precisely to the fact that equality, being a category of the abstract, cannot be transferred to the realm of beings without becoming a lie and, in consequence, without giving rise to contemporary inequalities which surpass any that have been ever seen under non-democratic systems. Here, too, it is war which supervenes, but in forms under which it is not even recognized as such any more, since it is in fact the systematic crushing of millions of beings reduced to a total impotence.

We should never cease to recall to ourselves that a world in which millions, in which tens of millions, of beings have been reduced to slavery cannot be considered as a world at peace; but, on the other hand, whatever may be said to the contrary, a condition of iniquity of this sort is radically different from anything that may have existed at a time when the fundamental principles of law and human rights had neither been proclaimed nor even thought of. The most scandalous aspect of the present state of affairs, for anybody who reflects at all, is precisely the intolerable contradiction between these principles of human right which nobody has quite the courage to make a formal argument against and the systematic violation of the most elementary actual rights. Our most serious problem is that of discovering how such a contradiction is possible—possible as a matter of actual experience, not as a mere mental notion. But what I have been trying to show is that it is precisely the intervention of the spirit of abstraction, considered as a kind of disease of the intelligence, that makes this contradiction possible. And yet the expression 'disease of the intelligence' does not, perhaps, convey my meaning quite exactly. For the spirit of abstraction has its origins in the passions. We should have therefore to probe rather deeper to discover what are the real sources of what looks on the surface like a disease of the intelligence; but that would demand another investigation, which we cannot embark on now.

CHAPTER IV

THE CRISIS OF VALUES IN THE CONTEMPORARY WORLD

WHAT exactly are we to understand by a 'crisis of values?' The terrible spiritual unease from which mankind is suffering—I am speaking, of course, particularly of Europe and Asia, but possibly also of America in so far as that continent has still direct ties with Europe—has to do with the fact that a kind of massive transformation of values is taking place for mankind, or what, more simply, one might call a complete change of spiritual horizon. Thus it is that some people are able to fancy that the convulsions of which we have been the terrified witnesses can be explained by the coming into being of a planetary or cosmic consciousness; these horrors are in some sense the price mankind has to pay for establishing himself on a new and superior level.

I must say here that this way of looking at things seems to me to involve the most dangerous of illusions; and there can be no doubt that it implies a total failure to grasp what values really are, or rather what reality is. For what we call values are perhaps only a kind of refraction of reality, like the rainbow colours that emerge from a prism when white light is passed through it. The men of whom I am thinking—and some still believe themselves Christians, though they have flung overboard without really being aware of it a good part of the Christian heritage and message—to all appearances have let themselves be dazzled by the mirage of space and time. In astronomy particularly, on the one hand, in the developments of what is rather rashly called the science of prehistory, on the other, they think they see the signs of a real spiritual advance to a higher level. But does this attitude not presuppose a postulate which they see no need to make explicit, and which experience does seem flatly to deny? This postulate, which does not lend itself very easily, however, because of its massive character, to precise formulation, is that the startling development in our time of such knowledge, or of what I have elsewhere called *homo spectans*, man as a spectator, can only have been carried out on the basis of growingly ample and profound spiritual foundations. But this postulate is not true and is not even plausible. There is no valid reason for supposing that a scientist, whatever his special subject may be, should not be in his essential nature a creature of almost absolute poverty, of, I would even say, almost absolute unworthiness; perhaps wholly given over to greed and ambition or, what is worse, wholly lacking in love, in charity. I recognize willingly that where a very great mind is in question it is hard to suppose that this is the case. But has a great scientist necessarily a great mind in this sense? Surely not, and it is not even the case that the man who has a great mind has always necessarily a great character; it is by no means certain, for instance, that Leibniz and Hegel had great characters. At least there is no synthetic *a priori* connection between greatness of mind and character.

I will add that, even supposing that in the case of the great scientist—in so far as he is a seeker or a creator—this connection between greatness of mind and of character may in fact in the largest number of cases really exist, still, even so, that would apply only to the scientist himself: not at all to the innumerable individuals who, at a popularized and debased level, profit from the work that the scientist has carried out. The most serious error or the worst deficiency of the cult of science for its own sake lies in this failure of men to ask themselves what becomes of science, or how not so much science itself but particular scientific truths degenerate, when they are taught to people who have in no sense taken a share in the asceticism or in the conquests of science itself. People have carefully avoided noticing the degradation which truth suffers when it is transmitted in this popularized form; and above all the insufferable pretensions which it gives rise to just where it is least living, where it is almost totally uprooted, where it is in no sense the reward gained by a really heroic sacrifice.

However little we may reflect on the subject, everything

does lead us to believe that the whole notion of a 'world consciousness', and of the values attached to that consciousness, is a mere fiction; but it is a matter of capital importance that we should ask ourselves just why this is so. In recent writings of mine I have attempted to show that at the foundations of these new ethics we find the mirage of a false unity. Quite generally, we can say that the notion of unity has not been worked on hard enough, and that people have not been wary enough of thinking of unity in a way which is fundamentally quite materialistic. One could exemplify this point in many ways; but simply to grasp it we have only to look at the concrete situation in front of us and at the processes of apparent unification that have been set going in the contemporary world.

Here, for instance, in a country like France ruled by a more or less socialist government, are people who eat the same food, wear the same sort of clothes, read the same papers, listen to the same programmes on the radio. It is of course very possible that in the long run these people will all become rather like each other—even if, during a period of transition, because of their temperaments, their former experience, their heredity, they no doubt react in diverse fashions to the conditions of a standardized existence. But let us allow that they do come to resemble each other to the point of becoming, so to say, interchangeable: has one the right in such a case to speak of unity? We are in the presence here of an equivocation which must be exposed. *Identity does not mean unity*: or rather, even supposing that a real unification is in process here, it will be a unification by reduction, a unification through the loss of those differences which, to begin with, conferred on the people concerned their individuality, their value. Far from its being the case that the kind of unification towards which we may be tending is itself a positive value, it is in fact a unification that can be carried out only *by sacrificing existing values*. We may say that such a unity or rather such an identity is *the opposite of value*.

But the truth is that people have so far neglected to ask the key question, which is just this: under what conditions, and from what point of view, *can* unity be thought of as a value?

And it is just here that any reference, whether explicit or not, to the methods of mathematics or physics can lead us only into the most dangerous errors. I have in mind here, of course, the example of elements being added to each other or combined with one another to form a larger whole. If we cling, in our thinking about man's unity, to the level of addition of units to one another or even to that of some objectively conceived synthesis of elements, we shall not be able to get beyond a realm of discourse that must be considered as in itself indifferent or foreign to the idea of value. It is all too clear that the situation, in regard to unity, is transformed and very much complicated as soon as the idea of consciousness is taken into account.

However, let us walk warily here: let us be on our guard against the kind of crude fantasy that postulates, for instance, elements called A and B, each endowed with consciousness (C being the consciousness of A, C′ the consciousness of B), and a whole constituted by the elements A and B, taken somehow together, and itself endowed with a consciousness which we can call C″; for things as they actually are will simply not allow themselves to be represented in this way: this consciousness C″, which is itself a synthesis of the consciousness C and C′, is a mere fiction, and one against which French sociological writers have not always been sufficiently on guard. In fact there is no meaning at all in the supposition that a sort of totalization, a group combination, of consciousnesses can really take place. What is true is that if A and B decide to group or to associate their resources, that combination of their resources will necessarily express itself as an increase of their power. In such a case C, the consciousness of A, may very well experience a certain satisfaction at this increase of power, and it will be the same with C′, the consciousness of B. It may be also that the consciousness of this increase of power takes on an obsessional character, and that A and B in some sense coincide in their obsessions. But this coincidence will almost certainly imply, as a kind of counterbalance, some sort of loss (let us say, for example, a narrowing of the field of vision) both for A and B. Both will change, and change for the worse—there will be an alteration in their conditions, in the bad, and in fact pathological, sense in which the word *altération* is used in French: a deterioration. One should add that A runs the risk of appearing to B, and of course B to A, as a simple means of acquiring this feeling of increased power. This amounts to saying that neither of them will consider his partner as a being endowed with a dignity and reality of his own. But have we not a sound basis for thinking that a genuine unity, a unity that would be a value, could only be brought about on condition that this dignity, this reality were properly recognized, as they are where an intimate relationship—real affection, friendship, love—has been solidly established?

All this, however, has only taken us up to the entrance of our subject, under a sort of portico which we must now pass through. But we can all pass through it on condition that we make a direct attack on the very idea of value: only, *is* value really an idea? In all that follows, I shall start from the hypothesis that something was irremediably compromised, if not actually lost for good, from the moment when the very notion of value made its appearance in philosophy. I emphasize the words 'in philosophy': I am not thinking here of Political Economy which, of course, could not fail to imply a technical investigation into the nature of values. But has the mistake of philosophers not been that of transferring, by a process of illicit extrapolation, into the realm of essences or of being a notion which in reality only properly relates to the empirical cycle of production, distribution, and consumption? And was their mistake not also that of assimilating, sometimes cynically, sometimes hypocritically, the man who devotes himself, for instance, to the quest for truth or the practice of goodness to the man whose place is somewhere on that economic circuit? Of course, if one keeps to the empirical data themselves, that assimilation can appear not only justified but almost inevitable. It can be truly said that Vermeer or Mozart have flung on the market material which has become wealth or a source of profit for picture dealers, exhibition organizers, editors, performers, impresarios, and so on. But everything is lost if we do not retain the sharpest possible awareness of the absolute transcendence of the 'View of Delft', 'The Woman in the Turban', the 'Symphony in C Minor' or one of the quartets, in relation to this possible economic exploitation of such works of art. However, as soon as we start using the term 'value' in strictly philosophical discourse, there is every reason to fear that the way is being paved towards such sinister confusions. I am thus led to make the no doubt paradoxical assertion that the introduction of the idea of value into philosophy, an idea almost foreign to the great metaphysicians of the past, is, as it were, a symptom of a kind of fundamental devaluation, a devaluation of reality itself. As often happens, the idea and the word together make their appearance as the marks of a kind of internal collapse, and what the word really seeks to indicate is the place where the collapse has taken place.

This becomes particularly clear when truth itself, as in Nietzsche, is treated as a value. But I should like to cite another kind of example of this very general phenomenon. It seems to me that the development in philosophy of what is called 'personalism'—the very word has become insupportable—would only have been possible in an increasingly dehumanized world, in which the reality of what one means by 'the person' is every day trampled underfoot.

It would be permissible, I think, to suppose that we are here in the presence of some process of compensation: an almost entirely illusory process, to be sure, since it seeks to reconstitute at the level of the ideal—or fundamentally at the level of the imaginary—what at the level of the real is tending on the contrary to be destroyed. People would not bother to appeal to the idea of 'the person' so constantly if human personality were not on the way towards its disappearance. At the political level, this sort of thing is just as striking; one example will be enough for me, that of the use made of the word 'democracy' by men who have made themselves the champions of a political system, Marxist Communism, which implies the suppression of all the liberties that give the word 'democracy' its only valuable associations. Of course, we should be within our rights here if we talked of imposture; but we ought to have the courage to recognize that, except in the cases of a few real scoundrels, this imposture is not really recognized as imposture by those who are guilty of it; what we are dealing with is, rather, really an illusion but one so deeply rooted that it would be chimerical, at least for the time being, to dream of making the man who feeds on the illusion aware that he is deceived.

On the basis of such observations, our problem changes its appearance; it can no longer be a question of substituting one system of values for another, as one might replace, for instance, one coinage by another, or one system of measurement by another. Such comparisons are basically wrong; and it is on this radical difference of kind between such notions of measurement and exchange on the one hand, and whatever recent philosophers have been trying to get at when they talked about 'values' on the other, that we ought now to insist. When we talk of a system of measures we imply at the same time that there is something to be measured; and that correlation, and that contrast, constitute our whole realm of discourse. It is too clear to need emphasizing that a system of measurement is essentially relative, since it is the object of an initial choice. But, whatever Sartre, for instance, may have imagined to the contrary—and this no doubt is a very serious error in his philosophy, one fraught with consequences—what philosophers call 'value' is essentially something which *does not allow itself to be chosen*. Or let us be more precise: why philosophers were wrong to use the word 'value' is that it does irresistibly evoke the ideas of objective measurement and prior choice, and yet what they sought to designate by the word is really something at a quite different level. It is on the essential nature of this 'something' that we now ought to concentrate our attention, though of course we must resist the temptation to think of it as really an object or a thing at all. There *is* a central point of view from which whatever it is that we improperly designate by the word 'value' ought to be considered; but we must arrive at that central point of view itself.

The 'View of Delft' of Vermeer and the 'Thirteenth Quartet' of Beethoven cannot be thought of except as responses to a sort of appeal. The appeal, however, hardly becomes aware of itself as such except according to the distinctness with which the responses develop; and yet the responses, at the same time, tend to mask the appeal. In this sense, I should tend to say that an appeal has proper existence only for metaphysical reflection. That, above all, means that it cannot be compared to an empirical and identifiable appeal—to some known person calling out to me aloud. There is literally no point at all in asking *who* made such an appeal: we are above the 'who' level—above, not below, I insist, and we certainly ought to distinguish carefully this suprapersonal level from the infrapersonal level, which is mere abstraction. I am thinking, for instance, of the infrapersonal level of official notices: 'It is forbidden to . . .', 'It is requested that . . .', and so on. There does exist a permanent and sinister temptation, which sociologists, for instance, can seldom resist, to identify or confuse the suprapersonal and infrapersonal levels.

Let us notice, however, that it is from every point of view extremely difficult for thought to grasp the suprapersonal directly: in seeking to make a concept of it, we convert it into an impersonal abstraction. As always in such cases, we must have recourse to second-level reflection: to a kind of thinking that becomes aware that our first attempt to grasp the suprapersonal in thought has involved a degradation of what we were trying to think about and, by becoming aware of this, frees itself from that degradation. The way is thus made clear for a discipline thanks to which we are permitted to turn back towards the principle of whatever it is that we mean by value, which principle can only be *being*. But all too certainly a very great danger threatens us here. It is that of substituting a mere word, a mouth-filling sonority, for the rich and palpitating experience of what we call, in our defective philosophical vocabulary, moral and aesthetic values. Merely to point out such a danger is, however, in some sense already to conjure it away: for we cannot really lose ourselves in abstract discussions about the intrinsic characteristics of Being—as if Being were a *thing*, capable of being contrasted with other things, which are only its appearances and manifestations. From this point of view, the philosophical term Ontology, the Science of Being, is an unsatisfactory one and runs the risk of encouraging regrettable misunderstandings. For Being is, quite fundamentally, not something which one can discuss. We can discuss only that which is *not* Being and thus, indirectly and humbly, map and mark out the tracks that lead towards Being, so long, that is, as we ourselves are still able to climb back by these tracks towards Being; for it is just as true to say of them that they put a distance between Being and ourselves or lead us away from Being.

I would sum up all this by saying that a philosophy of values, in so far as it becomes aware of itself and of the confusions to which it has given birth, and also of the secret urgent, inner need that animates it, is capable both of transcending itself and of pointing towards that which transcends it infinitely.

But one must add at once—and here we are touching the living nerve of our subject—that common thought to-day is setting its course in a precisely opposite direction. In particular, it often lets itself be fascinated by the categories which lie at the *lower limit* of that scale of degradation (and of possible re-ascension) to which I have just referred. It is at that lower limit, for instance, that the notions of function and output, in particular, lie. But one should make a preliminary distinction here: there would be no point in considering the notion of function, or even that of output as such, as evil notions in themselves. What we have to do with here is rather deviations or perversions of these ideas. An expression which is current in the United States may help us to get our bearings. It is a common saying there that some man or other is 'worth so many dollars'. Maurice Sachs in his *Sabbat* tells us that when he was giving a lecture at San Diego, on the Mexican frontier, the chairwoman introduced him in more or less the following terms: 'Ladies, I flatter myself that I have been able to introduce to you some of the greatest lecturers of our age, at the times in their lives before they had grown too wealthy and cost too much. For instance, we had Mr Sinclair Lewis, who is worth a thousand dollars a lecture to-day, at the time when he was only worth a hundred. And just so with Mr Dreiser . . . To-day, I have the honour of presenting Mr Sachs to you, whose lectures are worth only a hundred dollars each to him to-day, but I hope for his sake they will soon be worth a thousand; I say, for *his* sake, for we won't be rich enough to have him then'. Sachs adds, 'I was no longer in public, I was exposed on a shop counter'. We should emphasize here that the English word 'worth' really has the sense of 'value' and is directly related to the word *wert*, which in German is even the technical term for 'value'. Let us suppose that the lecturer in this anecdote gradually loses his voice, his value will diminish, and finally he will be 'worth nothing'. But value conceived in this way has obviously its place alongside the ideas of output and function.

Let us note also that, at least in the United States, a man can be 'worth a hundred thousand dollars', even if as a man he is worth nothing, so long as he can still sign a cheque for a hundred thousand dollars. Let us be accurate, however: it is not a matter of the physical possibility of tracing certain symbols on the paper, but of the fact that the paper on which these symbols are traced will be honoured by the bank. It would be useful to ponder at length on the type of relationship between moral and economic concepts, to all appearances a degraded one, that the word 'worth', the term 'value', masks in such extreme cases. The French technical term *actif*, meaning one's credit balance in contrast to *passif*, one's debit balance, is rather suggestive in this connection, since it seems to indicate an intimate or dynamic relationship between a man and the sum of money which he has it in his power to dispose of as he pleases (for if the money is in the hands of a trustee pending litigation I think one ought no longer strictly to speak of the credit balance as an *actif*).

Now, whatever appearances there may be to the contrary, there does not really exist any fundamental difference between the kind of attitude I have been evoking and that which consists of identifying a man's value or worth with his possible output. In this connection I recall a scarcely credible fact: as part of the carrying out of some administrative regulations, citizens in France filling in certain papers connected with their taxes were asked, at least in certain regions, to evaluate their own intellectual capital. For instance, it was supposed that an artist or a writer, basing himself on what he had earned in previous years, could make an accurate estimate of what he was likely to earn over several years to come. Let us notice that this request may, strictly speaking, have had some meaning in the case of those who write, so to say, to eat; and who in bad years and good years, unless they are interrupted by a serious illness, pound out their steady three sex shockers or detective thrillers; but as soon as the artistic conscience, the creative impulse, in any form at all, comes into the picture, the request does cease to have meaning; and what is sinister in the world that is taking shape before our eyes is this claim to measure the case of the superior by that of the inferior, to reduce the superior to the level of the inferior. Here as elsewhere the techniques of degradation are in the ascendant.

But let us now ask directly just what this reduction of the value of the individual to his probable output implies. It implies that the individual has no dignity of his own, as he would have, for example, if he were considered in relation to a God, a Creator, in whose image he was made. Man is no longer thought of except as a set of possibilities, among which, moreover, a choice must be made; do not let us entangle ourselves in the metaphysical but very real difficulty about who is to make this choice; for we shall not really clear up anything by bringing out the word 'freedom'. Is freedom merely one human possibility among others? To deny this, that is to say to recognize in man's freedom a kind of specific reality, a priority in relation to the carrying out of his possibilities, is to reintegrate, though in a rather uncertain and timid form, a metaphysical principle which those who think in this way originally intended to do without. It hardly seems possible, on the other hand, simply to include freedom among possibilities; in other words, to say that I can be free or not;

or at least this way of expressing things would imply a complete change in the point of view. The finally almost irresistible temptation will now be to make a clean sweep of freedoms, and to place *in things*, in circumstances themselves, the conditions that will ensure that one possibility rather than another becomes actual.

All that argument may look abstract, but it is in reality very simple. It will be held that if a given individual may, starting off in life, become either a great artist or a great criminal, still there is no point in imagining an inner freedom in him that would decide his development in one direction or the other: what we have to take account of is these external conditions of existence that in the long run may turn him into either a Debussy or a Landru. Of course, from this point of view, it does look as if the notion of possibility ought in the end to suffer the same fate as that of freedom, and leave us with a radical fatalism. But the acceptance of such a fatalism, is, let us note carefully, possible only if we totally deny the competence of the evidence of the human conscience for which choices, that is to say, possibilities, do exist. However, from this very point of view, the evidence of conscience—or, in a wider sense, of consciousness—will tend to be treated more and more as a negligible factor; and I may remark in passing that psychoanalysis will frequently be called in as an ally to reinforce the plea which it has been decided to make against conscience. Unless, indeed, as in the case of the author of *L'Etre et le Néant*, one sets out to demonstrate that man's conscience, or consciousness, is always insincere, even, and perhaps above all, when it develops what looks to itself like a will to sincerity.

But to whose credit are we going to pay in what we have thus withdrawn from consciousness and in the long run also from freedom? For Sartre's attempt seems to me condemned to failure; it does not seem that it can resist the assaults of contemporary materialism and, above all, of Marxism. I use that phrase 'to whose credit', that image from banking, deliberately. At this point in our argument, this is the aptest kind of comparison to hand. We are in the same sort of position as an accountant studying a balance-sheet, observing that a certain sum has been withdrawn from the credit column, and asking what has become of it, since even in that case it cannot have simply disappeared: and we have to note that the answer to our analogous question is of an incredible poverty. A kind of humanism, which owes its origins if not its essence to Nietzsche, sought to transfer to man certain attributes that formerly belonged to a God now declared to be dead: but is it still merely to man that these gifts are being transferred? It is at this point that there surges up, under its most tragic aspect, the central problem around which all these reflections of mine are poised. If we have the courage to pierce below the surface, below, that is especially to say, a sort of flattering verbiage, are we not induced to recognize that it is man himself, the very idea of man, that is decomposing before our eyes? To grasp this, all we have to do is to bring this long parenthesis to a close, and to develop what we have already been saying about function and output. Everything tends to show that, in what is very pretentiously called present-day civilization, it is the man whose output can be objectively calculated—as I showed just now, when dealing with the special case of the taxable earnings of the artist or man of letters—who is taken as the archetype: that is to say (and let us note this carefully) the man who by his type of activity seems to be most directly comparable to a kind of machine. One might say that it is starting with the machine, and in some sense on the model of the machine, that man at the present time is more and more commonly thought of, and one should remember that this is true also of, and is perhaps the essential truth about, Marxism: even though Marxism has undoubtedly its origins in a rebellious protest against the human condition in an industrialized world. Yet Marxism seems to have shown itself incapable of resisting the fascination exercised on it by the spectacle of this very world against which it first revolted. It is therefore quite as one would expect that, given such conditions, the genuinely creative man who sees things in terms of quality should find himself out of favour and even actively discredited.

But the evil is greater than this and has deeper roots. After all the producer, whether he is a miner or a metallurgist, does make a positive and necessary contribution to the human world. It is not so—at least, in the limiting case it is not so—for the clerk, the official, and this because of the unhealthy and in some sense cancerous conditions of the proliferation of officialdom in our day. The government official is beginning to seem more and more like something parasitic or verminous that is being bred out of society's decay. Everything to-day seems to tend towards a state of affairs in which the individual will not only be pestered by this officialdom, but, what is still more serious, caught up in it, asked, under the pressure of threats, to take his share in it. It is enough to think of the number of forms about taxes, insurance, compensation, and so on, that everybody now has to fill up every year, to recognize that we have been literally conscripted into an auxiliary bureaucracy. That is a strangely significant fact. If we think about it seriously, this is perhaps the only form in which what chimerical minds would regard as a progress towards unity has been really brought about. Under the German occupation, for that matter, we in France have been able to see just how far this process can be pushed, every individual being seemingly more and more easily reducible to an index card that can be sent to a central office and whose entries will determine the further treatment of the individual. A sanitary file, a judicial file, a file on payment of taxes, to be completed to-morrow perhaps by an estimate of character derived from handwriting analysis or facial measurements—in what is called an 'organized' society such papers will be sufficient to decide the final disposal of the individual, without any account being taken of his family ties, his deepest attachments, his spontaneous tastes, his sense of vocation. For that matter, the very word 'vocation' like the word 'heritage' will be more and more devaluated and finally no doubt the authorities will refuse to recognize anything in the words at all except the residual validity of a surviving superstition.

It seems to me very important to notice that the methods which our enemies used during the war in dealing with inhabitants of occupied countries, labour conscripts, or deportees, should be looked at from this point of view, and not as the monstrous and unnatural expression of a demoniac will. These methods were, rather, the premature but at bottom rigorously logical expression of a state of mind which all around us we can see becoming more and more general, and that, moreover, in countries where the majority must be thought free of that madness which is itself, nevertheless—as Chesterton for instance saw so clearly—only a rationality that has broken out of its proper bounds. The only thing that appears as in some sense superfluous, as implying an excess of horror, inexplicable in itself, and not fitting neatly into a logical system, is the sadism of certain kinds of torturer. But this, again, may be only a superficial view; we have certainly no clear notion of the conditions in which the sadistic mentality is developed; it may after all represent a kind of explosion of the irrational in a world of false rationality. But the fact, for instance, that certain poor wretches whose output had fallen below a given minimum were hurried away to the crematorium does not appear at all an irrational fact, if we start with certain premisses. If man is thought of on the model of a machine, it is quite according to the rules and it conforms to the principles of a healthy economy that when his output falls below the cost of his maintenance and when he is 'not worth repairing' (that is, not worth sending to hospital) because the cost of patching him up would be too much of a burden in proportion to any result to be expected from it, it is quite logical that he should be sent to the scrap heap like a worn-out car, thus allowing any still useful parts of him to be salvaged (as, if I am not mistaken, the Third Reich in wartime salvaged the fatty elements of corpses). If such attitudes and methods still appear monstrous and absurd to us, it is because we refuse to acknowledge that man really can be thought of on the model of a machine; that is a premise which we reject spontaneously and with horror; and it is well that we should do so, but a purely emotional reaction is not enough; we have to ask ourselves if we can translate our emotional reaction into terms of thought, for otherwise it will be all too easy for the doctrinaires of the new rationality to see in this emotional reaction only the residual life, the last kick, of an out-of-date and exhausted attitude of mind.

Besides all this, the question really has an extraordinary practical relevance. When I had a radio discussion with two biologists of a more or less materialist tendency, M. Jean Rostand and M. Marcel Prenant, I had a very strong and definite feeling that they either could not or would not state this problem. The lack of agreement between their emotional reactions and their mode of thinking did not seem to worry them, and I think that they were even unable to perceive it. One ought to bring in here, of course, that notion of insincerity or bad faith, which Sartre has done such good work in underlining, without necessarily being free from the fault himself. People of materialist tendencies do in fact refuse to recognize that if certain acts or practices still appear to us as open to condemnation, that is because we are living on a moral capital of feelings which for some time survive the positive ideas and beliefs which originally justified them. But we ought not to imagine that such a state of affairs has the least chance of lasting for very long. There is every indication that these feelings, deprived in some sense of their traditional function, like a church turned into a museum, are bound to disappear. This, for instance, is what is happening to the peasantry of certain regions of the centre and south-east of France, whose old manners and customs, as Gustave Thibon has shown in a forcible and gripping fashion, are undergoing actual destruction. I have noted down the terrifying evidence of a young priest who lives in one of these regions and who said to me, 'Nothing counts any more for the peasants except money and pleasures, they have become mere automata at the service of money and pleasure'. I observed to him that one had no right to speak of men as automata when they were undertaking anything as toilsome and arduous as labour on the land. But I immediately added, 'The fascination exercised by the towns and by office jobs on the peasantry can, alas, perhaps be partly explained by the almost wholly automatized character of such jobs, of such lives'.

For the rest, one can ask oneself whether this apparent obsession with money and pleasure which my friend spoke of was not, above all, a phenomenon resulting from fatigue. And here we touch on an idea which strikes me as one of the most important among all those which I am offering for the reader's consideration.

There is every reason to suppose that the extraordinary growth of the spirit of negation which we have witnessed in recent years, among men who quite literally no longer believe in anything, and—this is the point I want specially to emphasize—who are not tied to anything except money (and this at the very moment when the value of money is obviously becoming a fantasy value), there is every reason, I say, to suppose that this spirit of negation can be very largely explained by the inhuman conditions of work and living to which such men have been submitted since the two World Wars: conditions, of course, which have their repercussions on their families. On a scale without historical precedent, men in this century have experienced destruction and have also experienced the apparent uselessness of superhuman sacrifices: given these conditions, unless a man still adheres to some positive religious faith, on what is he going to lean, where is he going to rest his hope? It seems as if the very idea of a future were being abolished; one does not know whether one may not be wiped out to-morrow. In such a situation, 'Carpe diem' becomes the universal imperative; but it is all too easy to imagine what 'Carpe diem' implies at the level of a society which no longer knows anything of the refinements of ancient Epicureanism. The reduction of life to what is immediately lived—and that in a world in which technique is triumphing in the form of the radio, the cinema, and so on—can lead only to an almost unprecedented coarseness and vulgarity.

Here, of course, we ought to correct our general picture with plenty of specific, and no doubt often contrasting, examples. Let us take for instance, the peasant: it is the normal thing that his existence *should* have its bearings set towards the future, towards the harvest. So there is a growingly deep divorce, a violent disjunction, betwen what is implied in his traditional mode of life and the new attitudes and habits he is now acquiring. We ought to ask ourselves whether the progress of Communism in the French countryside is not the almost feverish expression of this living contradiction between the peasant's old traditions and his new desires, a contradiction which, at his level, is not likely to become easily aware of itself. But further analysis would enable us to recognize two separate elements in this unrest: on the one hand, among a chosen few, what is in itself a touching aspiration towards a better existence, a more worthy and as it were a renewed life; and on the other hand, and above all, resentment, envy. The condition of life of a workman or of many clerks and other subordinate employees would provide material for similar analyses. In particular, it would be very interesting to discover under what forms the future impinges on the consciousness of the clerk or the petty official; it is all too obvious that, apart from a few ambitious exceptions, the idea of eventually retiring with a small pension has come to replace that of a task to be accomplished. But it is doubtful whether one can exaggerate the impact of this idea of retirement on a man's very way of life, of conceiving the relation between himself and his life. Living is in danger of becoming a mere marking time while one is waiting—something petty and cautious, a diminished life. The mentality appropriate to the retirement one is looking forward to anticipates itself. The so-called active citizen is in virtual retirement already. It would, however, show a deep lack of understanding to treat such an attitude only in an ironical way, or to use it as a target for one's satirical gusto. For I think that such attitudes are, above all if one understands the very depths of them, of a nature to awaken a strong sense of pity. Let us leave aside the question of an actual wretchedness of poverty, which cannot be tolerated, and in fact probably will be tolerated less and less: for I do not believe that one is sinning by an excess of optimism in believing that, except in the event of some new disaster, such wretchedness is bound in the long run to disappear. Yet, even leaving actual wretchedness out of the argument, the condition of the majority of men does appear, to the reflective mind, pitiable in the extreme, from the moment when their horizon no longer stretches beyond the limits of this earthly life. And from this point of view we cannot be too severe in judging those who in the depths of their hearts have set themselves systematically to darken the human sky. But this whole theme would need a long elaboration, and we should have to emphasize, particularly, the impoverishment and even the adulteration which, for centuries past, the notion of truth has suffered.

The combined effect of all the remarks I have just been making is to show us that the human world to-day—a world some at least of whose principal characteristics Kafka has surely correctly grasped—is a world in great part given over to fatigue, and one suffering from a distress so deep that it no longer even recognizes itself as such. But at the same time—and this is the most terrible thing—a parasitic mode of thought finds very plausible ways of justifying this world: this mode of thought rests, at bottom, on a kind of idolatry of the masses and of the man who is at home in the masses: it lulls itself with the hope of seeing these masses, this man at the service of the masses, attaining a happiness which so far has been unknown and which, moreover, in its fulfilment will coincide with the fulfilment of social duty. Here again we have a formula of ancient philosophy rising up into new life; but it is no longer like 'Carpe diem' an injunction for immediate application, it is on the contrary the expression of a hope for which a long-term credit must be allowed: the hope that virtue and happiness are ultimately identical. Unhappily, experience must be our teacher here; what we can watch growing up around is in fact a mode of life in which the words 'virtue' and 'happiness' are tending to become emptied of all meaning. In a termite colony, for instance, there is no reason to suppose that there is anything which merits either of these names. But recently I have quite often had occasion to say that here we have what does seem to me a real possibility of choice for man: *between the termite colony and the Mystical Body:* and the gravest error that anybody could commit would be to confuse the one with the other. Yet, for a mind which is not at home with the terms of Christian mysticism, the expression 'Mystical Body' no doubt seems an almost meaningless one, and we shall have to make clear by concrete examples what we have in mind when we use this phrase.

At a level which is not the mere level of passing events, of news, the dominant fact about our world to-day is that life is no longer loved. Fundamentally, nothing can less resemble the love of life than an unhealthy taste for immediate enjoyment: in the indulgence of that taste, as I have said elsewhere, it is as if a kind of marriage tie between man and life had been broken. Moreover, it is extremely interesting to observe that the breaking of this tie coincided in history with the progressive establishment of biology as a science. And one may say, moreover, that the rupture between man and life has been observable in every circle in which a certain sense of the supernatural has not been preserved. For it is clear to-day that Nietzsche was guilty of a colossal error on this matter: that, I mean, of believing that Christians hate life, where, apart from certain heretical exceptions—I am thinking above all of Jansenism—it is exactly the opposite that is true. In particular, Nietzsche completely misconceived the meaning of the Christian belief in original sin: our awareness of original sin is our awareness of a principle of death that has found its way into the heart of our true life: redemption is the act by which God has grafted a new life—Life itself—on a life attacked by death, and which, without that grafting, would certainly be damned. The dominant question to-day is how these ties between man and life can be renewed, how the love of life can be rekindled in beings who no longer seem to have any feeling of it. But at this point we must avoid being the victims of certain very dangerous illusions. For it is obvious that our problem is not, fundamentally, that of reawakening a taste for life in a sick man by creating amusements for him. It is a much deeper, a more radical problem, and amusements and distractions are a completely inadequate solution; there is every reason on the contrary to suppose that current types of amusement, above all the cinema and the radio, where they are not guided by a higher principle, play into the hands of despair and death. Incidentally, let me add here, since I have brought up this idea of diversion, that Pascal, if we take him literally, seems to me on this subject an extremely dangerous guide.

It is not, therefore, in terms of value but only in terms of love that one can succeed in even stating this fundamental problem. But love is substantial, love is rooted in being, love is not commensurate with anything on which a value can be set or with anything 'marketable', as the English say; and possibly it is only a sufficiently deep reflection on the nature of love that will enable one to recognize what an impossibility a philosophy of values is. For love is not a value itself and yet, on the other hand, there is not and cannot be any value without love. But a metaphysic of love, allowing that it brings in, though no doubt without making it an absolute, the distinction which so many contemporary theologians have borrowed from the Swedish thinker, Nygren, between *eros* and *agape*, cannot fail to culminate in a doctrine of the Mystical Body.

I have now reached the end of the task which I set myself in this chapter and I must confine myself in conclusion to making what seem to me a few essentially relevant remarks.

In the first place it would be absurd, not to say crazy, to suppose that there exists some technique, that is, some combination of methods which can be defined in abstract terms, by means of which we could reawaken love in souls that appear dead. Quite summarily, we have to say that such a reawakening can only be the work of grace, that is, of something which is at the opposite pole to any sort of technique. But this observation ought not to lead us to despair or, what comes to the same thing, to shut ourselves up within a sort of quietism, that is to say, to put a grinding brake on the dynamic impulse that leads us to act, to will, to bring remedies. In fact, an objection to my argument that is based on the fear of this sort of quietism seems to me to imply the falsest possible notion of grace and the ties that bind grace to man's freedom. Here again, we ought to denounce the errors of Sartre and his school. But, in fact, these errors are more or less common to all contemporary non-Christian philosophers; and for this fact the old rationalist philosophies bear a heavy load of responsibility. In fact, as soon as I think of grace, of the transcendency of grace, that thought itself tends to be transmuted into a freedom at the service of grace. 'At the service', I say: but there is another word whose meaning is no longer understood. Through an incredible aberration, every kind of obedience tends to-day to be thought of in terms of passivity. Yet to serve means to expend oneself on behalf of something: the soul of service is generosity. The servant is the opposite of the slave. But our contemporary word-battle confounds these two terms. Here I can only point to the path on which that type of reflection which aims at reconstruction ought to set out; without this type of reflection, there is no philosophy worthy of the name. What we ought to ask ourselves is in what conditions freedom really can be exercised in the service of grace. There are two possibilities that we can immediately reject. In the first place, nobody can any longer accept the atomic individualism that was fashionable in the last century. This fact is too obvious to need insisting on. But the other possibility should be explored, mapped, and denounced with great care: I am speaking of the possibility of immersing oneself in the masses.

There is every reason to believe that it is only within very restricted groups, very small communities, that freedom can really be exercised in the service of grace. Such communities may assume very different forms: a parish, certainly, but also some straightforward business or professional undertaking, a school, for instance, but also for all I know an inn . . . One should add also that these groups should not be 'closed communities' in the Bergsonian sense, but on the contrary open to each other, and linked by tactful intermediaries, perhaps travelling from one community to another. Between these groups ties should grow up giving them the unity of grains in an ear of corn, but certainly not that of the mere elements lumped together in an aggregate. What we have to recreate is the living tissue. Not merely the national tissue. For we have got, I think, to look much further than the nation. It is not for that matter demonstrable that the nation, as such, can still constitute a quite living unity in the huge collective context we see around us. As Arnold Sandieu—in some matters truly a prophet—saw with penetrating clarity, we have to keep our eyes both on what lies on the far side and what lies on the near side of the national horizon.

These remarks, I can foresee, will provoke reactions of annoyance: among which I shall mention only this one—it will be said to me, 'We have no time, disaster threatens us'. I quite agree, disaster may be imminent. But no general scheme of action will enable us to conjure it away. Whether it must or must not happen, we should look further, beyond the possible deluge. And in this case, as in Noah's, it is only the rainbow of reconciliation that can bring salvation to us—though it may, of course, be salvation elsewhere: salvation far beyond our earthly limits, far beyond the unavoidable yet only apparent bankruptcy of our earthly deaths: in eternity: in an eternity whose call upon us becomes irresistible as soon as we have laid bare the mechanism of the triple illusion practised on us by the object, by number, and by value.

CHAPTER V

THE DEGRADATION OF THE IDEA OF SERVICE, AND THE DEPERSONALIZATION OF HUMAN RELATIONSHIPS

On one's first broad view of the matter, when talking of the notion of service it is tempting to bring in Hegel's dialectic of the Master and the Slave: but I believe that by doing so one would risk further complicating and obscuring an already by no means easy problem, and it is better, I think, to start, as I so often do, more or less on the ground floor: by considering the various related and yet distinct meanings which the word 'service' has in current speech and the idea of service in our thinking. Let us start then with the noun 'service' and the verb 'to serve.' In one extreme case, we can notice that 'service' means merely 'utility', 'to serve' merely 'to be put to a use': as for instance, when we say of some apparatus or machine: 'It no longer serves any purpose', 'I can't get any more service out of it'. But in the other extreme case the verb 'to serve' has overtones which seem foreign to the ideas of mere utility or utilization, as when one says, 'There is something honourable, something noble in serving'. When applied to a machine, or to man considered merely as a machine, these words obviously lose all meaning. Honour, nobility: these are words that presuppose a kind of inwardness or, more precisely, not only a conscience but an effort on the part of that conscience at self-justification. Just as two points on a flat piece of paper define a straight line, so these two extreme cases give us a kind of range or keyboard along which our analytic reflections about the nature of service will be able to exercise themselves profitably.

The idea of service can also give rise to certain observations which, though they are in no sense parallel with the preceding ones, reinforce and give greater precision to their scope. Service, one may say, is essentially the act of serving in the second sense which I have defined: but we should notice, on the other hand, that the word 'service' is being less and less applied to this act and more and more to the administrative centres carrying out certain definite social functions—'the social services': and services in this sense are more and more merely government offices.

On the basis of these quite elementary observations, let us fix our attention on some data about what I have called the contemporary attitude of mind.

Suppose somebody is engaging a servant and looking into his references. 'I see', he says, 'that you were in service with Mr So-and-so for a year. What exactly did your service consist of?'

Such phrases can be, and ought to be, interpreted in the first place in a purely functional sense. 'To serve' here means 'to be employed'. You were employed by such and such a person, what exactly did your employment consist of? It is interesting to notice that there is no fundamental difference, in his relationship to my point of view, my consciousness, between the man I am questioning and some apparatus which I am thinking of buying or renting: what preoccupies me first of all is to know what use this apparatus can be put to, how much wear and tear it has suffered, and I get in touch with the person who has had it in his hands before me, so as to ask him the questions which he is in a better position than anyone else to answer. Let us notice that what I have called inwardness is here, provisionally at least, left on one side. Perhaps, however, when I seek out and question my potential servant's former employer, this inwardness will reappear as one of the headings of my list of questions. After asking: 'Is this man clean? Is he careful?'—questions which, *mutatis mutandis*, could be applied by a slight transposition to a machine, to its accuracy of function—I shall perhaps ask: 'Is he a devoted servant?' And the answer I get may be merely this: 'That is hard to say, all I can affirm is that he does what he has to do very punctiliously'. This answer brackets off a secret, indeterminate, problematical zone, that of the feelings which the man whom I am thinking of taking into my service may or may not possess. In all this, we are still moving at the purely functional level. But it is very likely that this wary and prudent answer may awaken in me a certain uneasiness—if, at least, I conceive of service as an intersubjective relationship implying some kind of real exchange between two beings. What we must emphasize now is that when this intersubjective aspect of the problem crops up we leave, though under conditions which it is not very easy to make precise, the plane of mere function.

To grasp this point we must bear in mind the traditional idea of the servant, which is not at all that of a *servus* in the degraded sense of that word, of a slave. The servant, or at least the good servant, is distinguished by a kind of attachment; and it is into the deeper meaning of this in itself rather indistinct notion, attachment, that we must now look. It is above all important to point out that to the mere employee, in the exact and restrictive sense of that word, to the man who considers that he is paid for carrying out during a fixed and definite period of time some specific task, and that he owes his employer nothing over and above that time and the performance of that task, the very idea of attachment in this sense must be something foreign. I would even say that the idea of attachment excludes, of its very nature, the idea of this sort of strict and definite accountability. A quite characteristic example is furnished by the members of a hospital staff who, when they have completed their period of service during the course a day, do not hesitate to 'knock off', leaving the services which this or the other patient may be claiming of them uncompleted. They owe nothing beyond what they have already given. As for what remains to be done, if it is not exactly up to the sick man to look after himself and clear things up, which would be nonsense, it is up to the hospital administration to do what is necessary; for their part, they wash their hands of it.

From the point of view of the attitude of mind it implies, such a fact is very significant. On the one hand, the male or female nurse in question is assimilating himself or herself to a machine which has to produce a definite output over a definite period. On the other hand, we should notice that—by a paradox that demands all our attention—this habit of regarding oneself as a machine, which might seem a degrading one, has as its other side a kind of pretension: a pretentious idea of oneself based on the idea of contract. I owe only what I am paid for—when I have carried out the stipulations of my contract, I am my own master, nobody has the right to make any claim on me.

It is obvious that this attitude of mind, or let us say this mode of self-assertion, underlies a quite general contemporary phenomenon, the growing shortage of domestic servants. Those who in former days sought positions with private persons to-day prefer to earn a living in an office or factory. There are many factors that would have to enter into the explanation of this fact, among them a growing taste for collective life. And the phenomenon can find some justification in the scandalous way in which masters and mistresses—especially in the middle classes, and above all in the urban middle classes—did for such a long time treat their servants. These abuses, however, cannot be regarded as the real cause of the phenomenon we are considering—especially since there has been a complete change of manners in this sphere, and it is now, by a very understandable reversal, servants not masters who are able to take a high tone and exact a high price for what they have to offer.

The real problem, the one I touched on a short time ago, has to do with the nature and value of attachment: what is the basis of attachment and also what sort of feeling is it? Perhaps we should not exactly call it a 'feeling' at all: there seems to be every indication that attachment is somehow situated beyond or outside the psychological awareness of being attached that an individual can attain to. We have all known great-hearted servants who were nevertheless insupportable; whose frankness of speech took a most insulting form, and who in the daily detail of life behaved as if they felt only dislike and contempt for the people to whom nevertheless their whole existence was really devoted. It is important to notice that, in its most traditional forms, this attachment seems more often than not to have a supra-individual character: it was an attachment to a family or a dynasty (I emphasize the word dynasty, for here, certainly, are the sources of the dynastic sentiment). But we must not let ourselves be deceived by mere abstractions . . . I am not wrong, I think, in saying that for such servants the family or the dynasty becomes in some sense manifest in some typical individuality, which appears, as it were, its incarnation; there is every reason to suppose that such individualities become, for the servants who have been able to draw near to them, the source of a devotion to a mediocre or even unworthy progeny, a devotion sustained by the expectation of the birth some day of a grandson, say, who will again incarnate the family qualities. In this connection, I do not think one can over-emphasize the fact that among servants it is generally old people and children who arouse the most pure-hearted devotion. It seems to me for that matter that even in thought the old man and the child cannot easily be separated, that they make together an indissoluble duality in which one sees the mysterious unity of memory and hope becoming concrete. And this is eminently an ontological unity, a unity that transcends any notion of utility, of function. The old man is no longer any use for anything, and that is why he is venerable. The child cannot be put to any use either, or at least the utilization of children, as it was practised for instance at the beginning of the Industrial Revolution, to-day seems to us a crime, a sort of rape. To be sure, one can always consider the child as a future adult, as a possibility of carrying out functions, of producing an output. But these considerations are entirely foreign to the kind of devotion to a child which is felt here and now; and though the connection is very hard to grasp with conceptual precision, we feel a certainty that this attitude of reverence towards the present, towards present weakness, is directly linked to the sense of the eternal.

Thus a problem which we started discussing, as I said, at the ground floor level, at the level of the employment agency, as soon as we have begun to reflect on it with sufficient fervour transforms itself visibly into a problem whose metaphysical importance could not be too loudly proclaimed.

The world that is visibly taking shape before us is a world in which such attachment or devotion as I have been alluding to is tending to become, in the strict sense of the word, unthinkable; and if people do attempt to grasp these concepts, it will probably only be in order to condemn them. But in the name of what principle? Of what postulate? That is the question which we have now to consider.

But first, passing to the extreme case, I will say that this paradoxical idea of service, understood in its substantial sense and not, obviously, as the utilization of some piece of machinery, only takes on its real meaning when we acknowledge those aspects of the Fatherhood of God which are most disconcerting for what I may be perhaps permitted to call the everyday conscience. This disconcertingness seems to me to manifest itself above all in the fact that in its earthly symbols, God's Fatherhood takes on for us the guise of extreme weakness: the weakness of the old man or the child, precisely, the weakness of the poor or the sick. In making this statement, we are not making an exclusive use of Christian data, but also of pre-Christian data and of the religious experience that lies outside Christianity. I am strongly tempted to think the idea of service can reveal its full richness only when considered from such a point of view.

But we must at once acknowledge that this idea of there being something sacred in weakness, of human weakness being a symbol of divine strength, is—I have said this already and it is a point we shall have to come back to—profoundly ambiguous; that it can take on less and less religious, more and more profane forms in a world in which the feeling for personal or intersubjective relationships is becoming increasingly obscured.

As a teacher, I have at times had occasion to say to my pupils, 'Bureaucracy is evil, and it is essentially a metaphysical evil': what we have to ask ourselves now is what becomes of the idea of service in a bureaucratic world. In passing, I will note that it would be extremely interesting to investigate why it is that even service in the army tends to become degraded in so far as it becomes service in an administrative headquarters; for at that administrative level the hierarchical relationships of army life tend to lose their proper character. There is material in this subject for many precise and instructive observations, and it would be sufficient for our purpose to compare the peace-time with the war-time army, and also to compare, when the army is at war, the human ties that come into being in a fighting unit with those at rear headquarters: relationships at such headquarters tend almost inevitably to become distant, hostile, and I would even almost say, contemptible, just in so far as the members of such units are not caught up in the daily dangers or ordeals undergone side by side. Let me add in parenthesis that there is every reason to suppose that the excessive and unhealthy development brought about in the military machine, on its administrative side, by the late war, will prove to have exercised an almost entirely evil effect on human relationships and to have played a considerable part in bringing into being those new conditions of life of which almost all of us complain. I wonder if the French Socialists, who were anti-militarists in the past and are perhaps still anti-militarists to-day, have ever taken account of the fact that it is the institution they loathe, the Army, that may prove to have made the most effective contribution to the socialization of life: and that in conditions which constitute the most frightful possible threat to integrity.

It is important, however, at this point to be ready for an objection whose force ought not to be underestimated. It might take the following form: 'Is it not futile to regret the disappearance of a type of human bond that is linked to social forms which are historically exhausted? Was not the attachment of a servant to the family that employed him like a survival of feudalism in a world that had no more room for it? If people to-day devote their hearts, not to an individual or a family, but to an idea or a cause, does not that somehow mark real progress, a real step towards a mode of existence that will be more detached from servitude to the immediate? From this point of view are there not grounds, after all, for thinking that the employee has his being on a higher plane than the domestic servant?'

I shall leave the first part of this objection aside: merely remarking that the phrase 'historically exhausted' is one that should be used with extreme caution. What I should like to consider is rather the notion that the growing depersonalization of human relationships may after all imply progress, imply a kind of sublimation. Here, it seems to me, we have to insist on a very important distinction, that which I have already mentioned between the infrapersonal and the suprapersonal levels. But one should add that in concrete instances the making of this distinction may run up against many difficulties, and that the term 'depersonalization' is inconvenient in that it favours precisely that confusion we are anxious to avoid. Has, in fact, the employee who is a tiny cog in an great administrative machine normally the sense of serving a cause, a suprapersonal principle? The answer to this question can only be a negative one. Apart from some exceptional cases which we need not take into account, we cannot seriously maintain that such an employee has a consciousness of serving, in the precise and noble sense of the word: by that I mean above all that he can hardly know what the honour of serving is. Here, again, are the words 'honour', 'nobility' which figured at the beginning our argument.

Let us admit that these words almost startle us by their superannuated ring. What they irresistibly make us think of is the Army, what the Army is or what it has been for many people. But it is possible that we ought to be speaking only of the past. For, to the degree to which the Army has become industrialized and more and more dependent on the factory and the laboratory, the type of human relationship to which military honour came as a crown can hardly have failed to fall away from its old nature. Such honour was linked to sacrifice, to the struggle which the spirit of sacrifice welcomes and commands. But in a great administrative organization, whether we think of a Ministry, a Bank, or an Insurance Company, the elements of sacrifice and struggle can survive only under degraded forms. One can, of course, conceive that there may exist betwen the head of a department and his subordinates a personal tie built up through their loyalty and his kindness; but there is every reason to fear that this is a only superimposed phenomenon that in no way, or almost no way, affects the deeper structure or development of the organization. For it is also perfectly possible—and, as we know too well, it is much more than a mere possibility—that the employees are kept in their place only by the fear of being sacked or of sanctions which may range from fines to deportation; just as, on the other hand, they can be stimulated by the hope of promotion or a bonus. Such sanctions and stimulations 'work', of course, but they do not transcend the level of the infra-personal, and it is very clear that the concept of honour is linked precisely *to* personality or to what transcends personality; personality, for that matter, has existence only on condition of transcending itself, or of supporting itself on something that transcends it.

One must fear that, wherever the technocratic attitude of mind gains strength, so will this evil of depersonalization: obviously, there will be sporadic reactions against it, but it does seem that at the present time they can only have a very limited scope. The real problem is that of knowing to what degree an administrative machine can be informed with spiritual values; and it is very hard not to feel very pessimistic when dealing with this problem. There seems to be a chance of a positive solution only in the case in which what looks from the outside like a mere administrative machine in reality conceals a structure of a quite different sort, founded on values experienced and recognized as such. And obviously this *is* a possibility where the enterprise we are thinking of is something of limited size, not transcending the possibilities of concrete grasp and discernment, whether of the individual mind, or of a small team of men of good will who have intimate links with each other.

But the organizational giantism which technocracy seems inevitably to imply excludes precisely these humanizing conditions. And one does not see at all clearly how really gigantic organizations are to be informed with spiritual values. The very word 'spiritual' here loses its meaning. And what is perhaps most tragic in the world which is visibly taking shape before us is the coming to light of a kind of reality which has, after all, been born from human thought, but which seems as it were to have fallen away from thought, and to be antagonistic to all the initiatives of the living mind. Is this opposition between the world of techniques and the spirit a fiction? Something in us does affirm that it must and can be transcended, that it is not an irreducible opposition. But, frankly speaking—and after all our first duty in such matters is to be absolutely sincere—I do not see how this assurance could become solidly embodied; it remains at the level of desire or protest; it has not the prophetic character which belongs to hope and faith. I have said repeatedly already that I cannot by any means succeed in adopting on my own account the optimism of those who hypnotize themselves about the coming of a world consciousness. That optimism seems to me something foreign to the specific nature of the religious consciousness; it premises the possibility of a kind of syncretism, a blending of different and apparently inconsistent doctrines, in the bosom of which science and religion would be fused into the most hybrid of unities; and about the possible acceptance of any such syncretism one must have infinite reserves.

It seems to me obvious that if one attends only to the data of reason, or, fundamentally, to a mere estimate of probabilities, one cannot help seeing us as being dragged towards catastrophe: towards the fall of the Tower of Babel, by which I mean towards such a large-scale destruction of our industrialized world that the few survivors will have to start from nothing, in nakedness and faith: indeed, in the nakedness *of* faith.

And yet this catastrophism does, it seems to me, admit of one slight qualification: we ought not to accept such prophecies in a complacent spirit and there is even, mysteriously written in the depths of our being, an obligation to reject them. In my plays, in relation to quite concrete situations, I have several times put my emphasis on what I later defined as the duty of non-anticipation. What is true for each of us within the narrow yet inexplicable limits of his own life is true *a fortiori* for the human world considered as a whole. I cannot withdraw any of my objections to an optimism obviously profoundly incompatible with our condition as sinful creatures. Yet it remains our duty to act as believers; as men, that is, who believe in the miracle, and for whom human action at all times ought to be ordered in relation to miracle or *parousia*. Only, from our point of view, what is the practical significance of this duty or this demand?

I think that I should be formulating my thoughts fairly exactly if I said that each of us has a duty to multiply as much as possible around him the bonds between being and being, and also to fight as actively as possible against the kind of devouring anonymity that proliferates around us like a cancerous tissue. But these bonds between being and being that I am speaking of cannot be anything else than what has traditionally been called 'fraternity'. It is as illuminated by the notion of fraternity that that of service, to-day, can develop all its concrete richness. But one very important remark must be made here; we have to renounce for good and all the irrational and unmotivated connection which, at the time of the French Revolution, certain thinkers, wholly lacking in the power of reflection, attempted to establish between fraternity and equality. In France at least we have become so used to seeing the words 'equality' and 'fraternity' linked together, that we do not even ask ourselves whether the meanings of the two words are compatible with each other. Yet a very little reflection would enable us to recognize that the two ideas correspond to, as Rilke might have put it, contrary directions of the heart. The notion of equality expresses a kind of spontaneous self-assertion which is that of pretension and resentment: 'I am your equal, I am just as good as you'. In other words, the notion of equality is centred on a human consciousness claiming its own rights. Fraternity, on the other hand, is centred on the other person: 'You are my brother'. It is just as if one's consciousness projected itself towards the other person, towards my neighbour. This wonderful word 'neighbour' is one of those which the philosophic mind has too much rejected, leaving it rather disdainfully to the preachers. But when I do strongly think of another man as 'my brother' or 'my neighbour' I am not at all anxious to know whether I am or am not his equal, just because my thought is not at all clenched, in its purpose, upon the question of what *I* am or what *I* am worth. One might even say that the spirit of comparison is something foreign to the consciousness of fraternity. So true is this that if I have the consciousness of fraternity I can feel a genuine joy, which, *pace* M. Sartre and his followers, has nothing nastily masochistic about it, in recognizing the superiority of my brother to myself. It may be objected that nevertheless such a recognition of superiority may imply some sort of comparison. But it seems to me that a subtle qualification comes in here. The feeling of another's superiority which is accompanied by joy is of the order of admiration; it is something thrusting, impetuous, creative. Comparison is something quite different; and for that matter we have all also experienced the kind of sudden coldness or contraction that comes over us when, after having been carried away by admiration, or delighted sympathy, for the brilliant success achieved by a friend, we have had a sharp re-awareness of our own lack of success, our personal disappointments; but if there is the slightest touch of nobility in our souls, that painful contraction appears to us as something blameworthy, as a kind of treason, and we may say the same of the kind of spite with which we may perhaps tell ourselves: 'After all, I'm just as good as he is'. This is to say that the sentiment of equality as something experienced—as *Erlebnis*, to use the more expressive German term—is the counterpart of a kind of turning in on ourselves which works in the opposite direction of any kind of creative generosity. To be sure, one can rationalize this idea of equality, refine it superficially as one refines sugar, and forget its base origins; but I think that such refinement can only be the work of an attitude of conscious insincerity which it is the duty of reflection to denounce and destroy. To say to another person: 'You are my equal', is really to place oneself outside the actual conditions which make concrete apprehension possible for such beings as ourselves. Unless, of course, one merely means to say: 'You have the same rights as myself', which is a merely juridical and pragmatic formula, whose metaphysical content it is almost impossible to elucidate.

But it is obvious that these observations link us with what I was saying in the earlier part of this chapter. It is precisely in the name of an inward-turned and self-centred conception of equality that people claim the right to-day to rise in rebellion against the idea of service. In that way, we turn our backs on the possibility of real fraternity, that is, on every possibility of humanizing our relations with our fellow men.

And here a wide horizon opens out before us; we should have to ask ourselves how it was that, on the basis of what after all was naively taken as an *ideal* of equality, the shocking iniquities which we have witnessed were able to develop. There can be no question, of course, of claiming that iniquity—that a lack of equity, a lack of justice—did not hold sway before the coming of egalitarian ideas. What we must say is simply this, that the sort of ideological camouflage which covers up a fundamental lack of equity to-day renders it, if possible, even more hideous, and above all endangers and diminishes the real possibility of struggling against such injustice.

And here we come upon an unexpected and yet central aspect of our theme. To serve, in the valuable senses of the word, implies above all to serve truth, and perhaps it is by the help of this illumination that we can best perceive what it is to serve in the absolute sense of the word, that is, to serve God. But it must be admitted that at this point a very long and careful analysis would be necessary. If one clings to a certain traditional way of conceiving truth, which still survives in a number of rationalist or for that matter of Thomist teaching centres, it is impossible to understand how it should be that truth needs any service; from this point of view, there simply *is* truth, it is up to us to recognize truth, but truth is in itself completely unaffected by our recognition. Now the idea of such an indifference on the part of what one is serving is incompatible with the idea of service. And thus one is led to envisage a truth which, in some sense, has need of us, of the act by which we put ourselves at its service; we should have to investigate—and here we are touching on the borders of metaphysics—just what characteristics truth, conceived in this way, would have to possess so that it would not be absurd to think that it had need of us. Obviously we should have to admit that such a truth is mind or spirit, that it is *a* mind or spirit, but that it is in some sense in the process of incarnation, or more exactly that it is at once far beyond, and deeply within, that which we are ourselves. According to one's religious point of view, one will be led to see in this fact either a paradox or a mystery. Personally, I prefer to speak of the mystery of truth and it is, I think, within the Christian religion that this mystery best reveals its clarifying power. At least nowhere better than in a focal region such as the Christian religion can the value of the idea of service, transcending or stretching across the divisions of Christianity, be adequately emphasized. It is not and it certainly cannot be mere chance, if a world, taking shape around us, in which the ideas of attachment and fidelity are more and more being cheapened, at the same time is a world in which the lie in its most insulting, most aggressive forms is lording it over all kinds of critical thought. So far is it from being chance, that, on the contrary, there is a connection between the decline of fidelity and the growing power of the lie, whose basic principle I think reflective thought ought to be able to lay bare.

PART THREE

CHAPTER I

PESSIMISM AND THE ESCHATOLOGICAL CONSCIOUSNESS

A FEW months ago I was talking to Max Picard, the author of *L'Homme du Néant*, by the shores of Lake Lugano, and I shall never forget the calm way in which he said, at a turning point in the conversation: 'I am convinced that we are at the end of history. It is probable that there are many among us who will witness the apocalyptic event that will bring it to a conclusion'. Max Picard, as is well known, is a Catholic. But more recently still I heard a Protestant, Pastor Dallière, express himself in an identical fashion. In both men—and it would be hard to imagine two men of more contrasting temperaments—there was the same certitude of the coming of the *Parousia*. What specially strikes me is that, though one is a Catholic and the other a Protestant, neither is a man of sectarian mind; on the contrary they have both what I would call an exemplary awareness of the ecumenicity, the universal mission, of the Church. It is in relation to this eschatological affirmation of Picard and Daillière that the reflections I wish to present here will be arranged. (Eschatology in Christian theology is the doctrine of the last things, death, judgment, heaven, and hell.)

As a first step, I think it may be useful to face the immediate objection which a belief in the imminent end of what we call the world is likely to arouse among many Christians who are caught up in the life of this century and who are fighting as well as they can against the injustices and miseries of all kinds that to-day afflict our sight. Is not this eschatological affirmation, they may be inclined to ask, an example of escapist thinking: of the kind of thinking that distracts us from our immediate duties? If in a very short time everything is going to come to an end, shall we not be tempted to think that nothing has any longer any practical importance? Will there not be an irresistible impulse for us to shut ourselves up in a mood of expectancy, perhaps an anguished and feverish mood, perhaps a joyous and serene one, but in any case a mood which by its nature shuts us off from any kind of effective action in the world? From such a point of view the act by which we would abandon ourselves without restraint to a confidence that the Lord will soon come may be regarded as an act of desertion.

It seems to me that this objection, however much apparent force it has, conceals a number of rather serious confusions. It has a close kinship with something which I remember a Swiss Protestant lady, of rather limited intelligence, saying against monks and nuns who have chosen a contemplative life. It was precisely as deserters that she spoke of monks and nuns, accusing them of slipping away from the most urgent human tasks and fleeing to the shelter of a useless existence, an existence protected and shut off from life. If she had gone a very little further, she would have been treating them as mere impostors. Now the absurdity of such an evaluation of the contemplative life does not need to be demonstrated. Yet it has a kind of tangential value in that it does recall to us certain temptations to which we are, after all, exposed, as soon as we begin to take something for a vocation which may after all be only a kind of spirit of indulgence towards ourselves. In the same way, we should always be on our guard against what I should like to call an eschatological quietism, a quietism which is in direct contradiction to the message with which the Church has been entrusted.

But looking at the matter in a much more general way, one cannot disguise from oneself the fact that the very idea of an end of time, of time coming to an end, of an *eschaton*, is profoundly repellent to a certain type of mental attitude, widely diffused among Christians themselves, and of which we ought to try to get a distinct notion. It will be readily admitted that this idea does smack of a certain obscurantist pessimism, which is one of our legacies from the Middle Ages, and which is always in danger of coming to the surface again on the occasion of one of these passing crises or calamities which mankind so often undergoes. From this point of view people will be inclined to assimilate eschatological affirmations to those dark and sinister and more or less delirious ideas which seize the imagination when it is under the influence of some disease or some kind of intoxication. In taking up this attitude, of course, one postulates the existence of a contrast between the normal and healthy condition which allows man to form a true and relatively encouraging picture of his condition and destiny, and a pathological state which favours the development of such 'dark daydreams'. And I was certainly very struck, at a meeting which the Bergson Society held to discuss the general subject of techniques, with the way in such a respected philosopher as Edouard Le Roy sturdily refused to admit that there was anything in the present situation of humanity that had not already been met with on many other occasions. If one were to believe him, sound common sense compels us to believe that, once again, mankind will get to its feet again after recovering from its present grave sickness.

For my own part, I do not hestitate to say that it seems to me essential to take up the contrary position to Le Roy's. His position consists, at bottom, of proclaiming more or less explicitly that there is nothing to do but 'make a fresh start' and 'avoid crying over spilt milk'. I choose these expressions, with their almost aggressive air of platitude, because they express very vividly what one may call the dogmatism of the man who has 'made up his mind'. But it is important to notice that such a man and such a mind draw their calm certainties from a world that appears to them as normally constituted, though capable, of course, of being progressively guided towards a condition more conformable with the demands of a reasonable being. Here I can bear witness from my personal experience: this world, normally constituted, though capable of being improved in many of its aspects, was the world in which we lived at the end of the last century and the earliest years of this one. Now, it is not enough to say that that particular world is in ruins; we are perfectly well aware that it was not smashed to bits by accident, but that it carried within its own depths the principle of its destruction; and on this particular topic it would certainly be rash to deny *all* validity to the Marxian analysis. But an observation of this sort which brings *the depths* into view deals a mortal blow to the knowledge of himself which the man who has made up his mind, the man of settled opinions and attitudes, imagines he possesses; in the light of what we have lived through, his claim to self-awareness appears merely presumptuous. *In the light of what we have lived through*, I say, for it is just here that we enter a domain in which phrases about 'not crying over spilt milk', 'starting again as if nothing had happened', and so on, seem mere scandalous nonsense. For we have not merely gone through a harrowing experience, like somebody who has been the victim of an accident or has had a grave illness. We have been instructed by our harrowing experience. Something has been revealed to us, or at least ought to have been revealed to us; an abyss has opened under our feet. I am tempted to bring in the image of a volcanic eruption which reveals a central fire, whose existence was unsuspected, but which was there all the same, and is still there.

But it may be asked whether any kind of historicism, and particularly Marxist historicism, does not tend to have the very effect of blocking up our abyss-like awareness of this central fire—of this demoniac power, that is fundamentally to say—of which we ought to try to take account, it may be suggested, by using the methods of a generalized psychoanalysis and referring to the 'collective imagination' or other entities of that sort. Here again we are in the presence of the man of settled mind who is now granting himself a certificate of immunity from various kinds of delirium and aberration whose origins he will attempt to describe. This is the claim, the postulate, that underlies all scientific, literary, and philosophic conferences: 'Those of us who are gathered here, all of us reasonable beings and generally thought masters of our subject, have come together to discuss . . .' Obviously, at some levels of discourse, this claim cannot be criticized: urologists and heart-specialists have a real interest in meeting occasionally to exchange observations on localized and determinate pathological conditions, for which there are suitable special treatments. But the case is altered when such conferences deal with evils from which none among us can really regard himself as immune. In such cases, the attitude underlying such conferences, to the degree in which it implies an illusion about ourselves, a lie, appears more and more factitious and fundamentally open to condemnation. Let us notice, however, that it is just when such evils are extending their scope and striking deeper, that such desperate and fundamentally self-contradictory efforts tend fatally to multiply; and the too glaring and obvious failure which such conferences meet with can only intensify the despair that first gave birth to them. This is especially true at the political level, in so far as that can any longer really be dissociated from the economic level on the one hand, the moral and religious level on the other. And here we touch obliquely on an idea which seems to me an important one.

Optimistic minds seem to-day to find some comfort in the fact that a kind of world unity is visibly coming into being before us through the growth of modern techniques. But the real problem is whether a unification of this sort, whose chief expression is the elimination of distance, has a spiritual impact of any positive value; one cannot be at all certain that it has, and there is every reason to fear that international conferences and congresses, with all their sterility and speciousness, correspond precisely to this lying vision of a false unity.

The notion becomes fully clarified, I think, if one reflects even a little on what the nature of a real spiritual unity would be. One may, of course, content oneself with making use of a ready-made idea; if instead one makes the effort to ask oneself what unity is, one discovers that the idea is irreducibly ambiguous, if not in itself, at least in its concrete applications. To say that two entities together make merely a single entity is to say that a sort of coalescence has taken place between them that does not allow us to consider them apart; originally distinct, they now form a whole which is only ideally separable into its two elements. But at this abstract level we can imagine several different cases; either this unification of two elements in a single whole has been brought about by a process of reduction, or not: if it has, then one of our two elements has lost some of its specific characteristics in order to merge with the other; unification is linked to the impoverishment of one element, of the other, or of both. If, on the contrary, there has been no process of reduction, it is theoretically possible that the coalescence has been brought about without either of the two elements being modified in any way. To be honest, I am not sure that this is possible even at the level of physics, and at the biological level it is almost certainly inconceivable; at the spiritual level it is not even imaginable. At that level, in fact, the very notion of coalescence does not seem to apply. It seems at a first glance as if spiritual unification could be brought about only by the creation of a whole which had new qualities and within which each contributing element was, as it were, renewed; yet in postulating such a synthesis we remain in practice well below the level of the unity we are envisaging. Strictly speaking, we could here once more take up Nygren's celebrated contrast, which I mentioned already, between *eros* and *agape*, and say that *eros*, above all when taken in its romantic sense, consists of an aspiration to merge one's being in another's, or perhaps rather to merge with the other in a higher—or undifferentiated—unity. *Agape*, on the contrary, transcends fusion, it can take place only in the world of beings—I would say 'in the world of persons', but that the term 'persons' since Kant's day has tended to take on too formal and juridical a sense; while the confused 'personalist movement' in contemporary philosophy does not seem to me to have restored its value . . . Thus, would the highest unity not be one created between beings capable of recognizing each other as different, but of loving one another in their very difference? Such a unity lies at the opposite pole from any attempt at reduction: for ultimately every reductive process robs the reduced components of certain specific, differentiating qualities.

But it should be observed that technical progress, in its concrete impact, has just such a reductive effect. It reduces human diversity to similarity: it has brought about an extraordinary levelling of groups and of customs. Yet this levelling, on the other hand, has been balanced by the growth of a spirit of separatist self-assertion—the self-justifying spirit in its most fundamentally hateful aspect: as Werner Schee writes in *Le Dard*, in the world around us to-day everyone tends to say: 'I'm no good, but neither is my neighbour'. It is glaringly obvious that such a process by which traditional differences are reduced to a common denominator can only breed resentment in the world. There are various ways in which one could illustrate this. Of course, modern ideologies and the slogans that embody them, Marxism, Fascism, and so on, have these modern technical methods at their disposal. Yet it is just as obvious, and we should ask ourselves why this is so, that an ideology cannot be a source and centre of love: in the deepest sense it cannot be a religion, but only a pseudo-religion or a counter-religion. These are the characteristics, in particular, of Communism: even though Communism may profit from a deceptive analogy between its own message and that of the Gospels; and even though it may be from this specious resemblance, of which many ignorant and simple-minded people have been dupes, that Communism derives some of its dynamic thrust. But I think there are a few simple statements that we need not hesitate to make at this point.

Ideology aspires to become propaganda—to become, that is to say, an automatic transmission of formulas electrically charged with a passion which is fundamentally that of hate (and fundamentally, also, hateful) and which can only embody itself on condition of being directed against some group of human beings chosen as scapegoats; the Jews, the Christians, the Freemasons, the *bourgeoisie*, as the case may be. But nothing is more striking to witness than the ease with which one scapegoat can be substituted for another.

Such propaganda has a difficult job when it seeks to influence the individual who possesses a critical sense. It even runs the risk of annoying him and putting him on the defensive. In the masses, on the other hand, it finds its chosen field of impact; and yet even to say that, is to say too little.

What we should say, rather, is that it is propaganda which tends to bring into being the masses as such: by diffusing among the individuals of whom it seeks to make one agglomeration, by passing its electric current through them the illusion that they can attain to a sort of mass-consciousness, and that the mass as such constitutes something more real and more valuable than its members taken separately.

Such propaganda makes use, of course, of the feeling of power which individuals experience when they see themselves gathered in great numbers around a single object. But the analogy with great religious assemblies is as misleading as possible. For in a religious assembly worthy of the name all attention is directed upon a kind of mysterious and transcendent reality. Here, on the contrary, the object of attention is a mere pretext, and fundamentally it is *itself* which the crowd is setting up as an idol. The incredible misunderstanding of some French sociologists of the earlier part of this century consisted, we may note in passing, in interpreting the essential nature of religion itself on the basis of this kind of religious degradation. The monster political rallies which have become so frequent in the last twenty or thirty years have precisely the purpose of encouraging this sort of collective *self-worship*, which, of course, by its very nature cannot recognize itself for what it is; for the skill of the organizers lies precisely in making sure that the pretext for self-worship should never be recognized as a *mere* pretext. In passing, let me say that I think the Churches are guilty of a very rash act when they think to help on their cause by means of public manifestations more or less exactly modelled on the kind of rallies of which I have been speaking; for such manifestations let loose uncontrollable forces, and there is every danger that these forces will work against the true faith.

One ought to mention here, once again, the temptation of great numbers. This is certainly one of the most formidable temptations with which modern man is acquainted. It belongs to the same order as the temptation of the prestige of statistics. One may say that at the present time no organized body is really able to keep away from statistics, not even a body whose purposes are entirely spiritual (one thinks, for instance, of parochial and diocesan statistics about numbers of communicants). One cannot repeat too often, I think, or insist too strongly, that it is only on condition that one rejects the fascination of numbers that one can hope to remain at the spiritual level, that is, at the level of truth. But it should be added that, in our world as we find it, everything seems to be working in the most visible and tyrannous way to persuade us to the contrary. An ethics of the lie is in the process of being elaborated which commands the individual to make himself as nothing in the face of that multitude of which he is only an insignificant and ephemeral unit.

This does not imply that we can, and obviously still less that we ought to, attempt to restore that nineteenth-century individualism for which the case has now so completely lapsed. That individualism found extremely various and indeed fundamentally incompatible expressions. In its case, also, there is an illusion to be denounced, as sinister as the illusion of numbers—and indeed, notably in contemporary Germany, it has often sinisterly allied itself with the illusion of numbers: I mean the biological illusion. One might say that everything that strikes us as weak, shaky, and also, of course, as evil in the work of Nietzsche has to do with the prestige which the concept of the biological held for him. If Nietzsche admired Dostoevsky, it was perhaps because his knowledge of Dostoevsky was so superficial? if he had read the great novels, he would either have recognized in Dostoevsky his most formidable antagonist, or he would have been converted, for it is probable that in Dostoevsky's case the temptation of the biological was more firmly surmounted than in that of any other thinker. And at the same time there is in Dostoevsky something which infinitely transcends the kind of individualism we still find in Ibsen, not to speak of Stirner and the anarchists.

Thus we are not trying to give an exalted idea of the individual who defies the masses, and in fact we are not trying to give an exalted idea of anybody. By indirect and sometimes dangerous paths we are seeking to scrutinize what I have called, in the title of this chapter, the eschatological consciousness: the consciousness of the last things. Such a consciousness can be defined, above all, negatively: by its categorical refusal to adhere to a philosophy of the masses based on the consideration of techniques, and on the support furnished by the latter to what it would no doubt be rash to call civilization. It can be defined also by an equally determined refusal to ally itself with the optimism of men of settled opinions and attitudes: the optimism which, no doubt without daring to subscribe to the frightening and ambitious theses of Hegel, takes up a half-way position and complacently supposes that, at the price of certain regrettable excesses, history is assuring the achievement of certain moderate demands, certain average ideals, in which demands and ideals the man of settled opinions and attitudes can recognize his own comfortable limitations.

But if we seek to consider this eschatological consciousness from a more positive point of view, we shall find that a tiny number of survivors from wartime extermination camps have evidence whose value can hardly be over-estimated. It is enough to remember that among the horrors of Auschwitz and other camps there were men like Jacques Levy, the parish priest of Pont-Aven, Edmond Michelet. But from the point of view which I am tending to adopt, we must face the question of whether such camps can be regarded as in some sense an anticipation, a sinister caricature, of the world to come. The general adoption to-day over a wider and wider portion of a continent which we thought of as civilized of certain totalitarian methods takes on, seen from this angle, a terribly revealing significance. Would not one essential aspect of the eschatological consciousness consist in recognizing this phenomenon in all its amplitude, in its specific reality, and in seeing clearly that one takes upon oneself the guilt of the liar when one claims to regard the atrocities of other centuries as being on all fours with the horrors we have witnessed ourselves? In these distant centuries, the fundamental principles of a humane social order had not yet been either recognized or proclaimed. To-day men systematically infringe principles which they are perfectly well aware of; even more, with an unparalleled impudence, the very men who are trampling these principles underfoot do not cease to invoke them and to lend their own authority to the ideas (democracy, liberty, and so on) of which the system of government they intend to bring into being will ensure the final ruin. I should like to add that, this being so, it is very suitable that the philosopher himself should try, by an effort of religious recollection, to gather again within himself everything that has been thus wasted, flung to the winds, profaned.

But it may be asked whether such a consciousness, with its flavour of evensong and the sense of the coming night, is properly speaking an eschatological consciousness, especially in the philosopher's case? Can the latter subscribe in all sincerity to the idea of a sort of suprahistoric event that will come, in some sense from outside, to put an end to history? There is much that one could say on this matter: quite summarily, I will say here that we are to-day witnessing a universal turning into problems of processes which, in former centuries, were regarded as carrying on by their own momentum, and at the same time these indefinitely multiplied problems of our own age seem to suggest or imply fewer and fewer solutions. Would it not be reasonable to say that, as soon as reflective thinking begins to attack, in order to disintegrate it, the very unity of lived experience—and by the phrase I mean above all the act of living and of giving life—and as soon as questions asking 'Why?' proliferate unduly, it somehow happens that even questions which merely ask 'How?' become progressively insoluble? A world in which somebody has been able to suggest the granting of a salary to the mother of a family is obviously a world where the very roots of life are poisoned. It is, of course, from this point of view, also, that the cult of the State appears as a major scourge. There is a mad illusion that forces men to unload on the State the burdens they are no longer capable of carrying themselves, so that the wearied and flagging State becomes a symbol of impotence disguised in the trappings of absolute power. It is as he proceeds along this line of argument that the philosopher, considering impartially what is going on around him, is led to ask himself whether we are not in fact after all coming towards the end of history, and whether the atom bomb is not a real symbol of a tendency driving our race to self-destruction. No doubt it is at quite another level that the idea of the *eschaton*, the end of things, as the Holy Book presents it to us, ought to be brought in. But we may ask ourselves whether the situation which I have tried to evoke in these pages is not, as it were, the sensuous and historic garment in which an event presents itself to us, which it belongs to faith alone, not certainly to grasp, but to have a presentiment of in its positive reality.

No doubt some of my readers will at this point attempt to force me back into my last ditch: and I shall be asked: 'Do you personally really in good faith and in all sincerity believe that this apocalyptic event is close at hand?' But I don't think it is possible to answer such a question with a simple yes or no. Because it belongs to my essential nature, as a creature who is imprisoned by the senses and by the world of habits and prejudices in which I am caught up, to be for ever divided, this self of mine that is a prisoner may reply; 'No, I don't believe it', and thereupon may abandon itself to mere despair or, with more and more difficulty, may take refuge in some optimistic thought, some 'Suppose, after all . . .' However, something happens here which is of decisive importance: it is that this self of mine which is a prisoner cannot declare in all sincerity that it is I. I have an awareness of not being reducible to this captive self; the self of love and of prayer proclaims itself as something distinct, even though between the self of love and prayer and the captive self there is something more than a mere co-habitation. And it is only this self of love and prayer that can become an eschatological consciousness. Moreover, even to this self of love and prayer it is not given to prophesy; it would be passing beyond the limits set to its condition if it were to prophesy. But the task that does belong to it is that of preparing for this event: like the condemned man tidying himself for the last time before going off to execution. But in reality such a preparation could have nothing funereal about it. On the contrary, it could not be carried out except in a spirit of joy—that joy of being at the same time one and divers, which belongs to the essential notion of a Church as such. Incomprehensible to the captive self, this joy is like the anticipated response to an appeal of which we may now have only a presentiment but which will become, do not let us doubt it, ever more distinct and more urgent—the appeal which the men of 'settled views' are condemned never to hear.

CHAPTER II

MAN AGAINST HISTORY

I AM a philosopher and a dramatist, and there can certainly be no question therefore of my risking anything resembling a prophecy. I have said already in so many words that between the thought of the philosopher and that of the prophet there can be no possible confusion. Fundamentally, the philosopher has only a single instrument at his disposal, and that instrument is reflection. For that matter, I would be far from denying, indeed I would heartily agree, that philosophical reflection has its source in what I have elsewhere called 'a blinded intuition'. But if one can talk of a blinded or blocked intuition, this signifies that intuition in the case of the philosopher cannot be directly formulated: as it can in the case of the poet and *a fortiori* of the prophet. In the philosopher's case intuition offers what one might call a hidden nourishment to a mode of reflection that can exercise itself only on common experience as that presents itself to a sincere mind.

My topic is precisely as follows: whatever hope we may retain and ought to retain to the very end, it is nevertheless true beyond all discussion that we have before us the possibility of a catastrophe, and there is every danger that this catastrophe may entail the disappearance of everything that gives life its value and its justification. The mere fact that such a possibility lies before us is something that ought to evoke in us a tragically serious examination of our consciences. It is towards such an examination that I should like to proceed.

I shall take as my point of departure the preface I wrote to the French edition of Virgil Gheorgiou's *The Twenty-Fifth Hour*. I recall the words of the character Trajan in that book: 'In the most recent phase of its development, Western civilization is no longer taking account of the individual and there seem no grounds for hoping that it will ever do so again. That society knows only a few of the dimensions of the individual, man in his wholeness considered as an individual no longer exists for it. The West has created a society which resembles a machine. It forces men to live in the heart of this society and to adapt themselves to the laws of the machine. When men come to resemble machines sufficiently to identify themselves with machines, then there will be no more men on the face of the earth'. And it is impossible not to mention also a book which appeared after *The Twenty-Fifth Hour* and for which I know that Virgil Gheorgiu like myself has a great admiration, George Orwell's *Ninteen Eighty-four*. That is a book which grips one with hallucinating power and which transcends in its scope all the other novels of anticipation that I know of, no doubt because it confines itself to presenting as a completed picture what already exists in almost all countries more or less at the stage of a rough sketch. I consider the fact that, in France at least, Orwell's novel had no great success as a rather serious comment on our state of mind; that fact can be explained, it seems to me, by a kind of deep-seated cowardice: men were afraid of seeing in the depths of Orwell's magic mirror the image of the world that will be our own world to-morrow, unless we have the courage to reject it and to risk even martyrdom in doing so.

But in many intellectual circles to-day there is a tendency to slide round this problem or to let oneself be pushed off one's course by the current. I do not think such a tendency can be too explicitly denounced. What I mean is that the value of the individual, or perhaps we should rather say of the person, as postulated in Gheorgiu's book and Orwell's, tends to-day to be surreptitiously brought into question: I do not mean among fanatics, but among intellectuals who, though they may believe in their own sincerity, in fact let themselves be intimidated by the verdicts, pronounced in the name of history, which can hardly stand up even to a surface examination. And it is just at this point that the examination of conscience, to which each of us ought to have recourse these days, ought to come in.

Nothing is more common to-day than to hear Marxists, particularly, denouncing any philosophy centring on the idea of 'the person' as a hypocritical expression of capitalist society's preoccupation with the safeguarding of its privileges, the real and selfish objects of this preoccupation being concealed behind a mask of universalism. We recognize here a type of sophistry which is widely diffused in our time, and of which not only the Stalinists are guilty; one runs against it very often also in Sartre. There can be no question of denying that the notions of the person and personal rights have often been used, in a superficial way and for partisan purposes, by men who were really inspired by the wish to oppress their neighbours for the benefit of their own caste or clique. But there is nothing in this fact which permits us to discredit in any way the ideas themselves, and we ought on the contrary to maintain that the ideas, in so far as they do not remain mere abstractions or reduce themselves to empty words, but attempt rather to embody themselves in customs and institutions, *do* constitute our only imaginable safeguard against a condition of technocratic barbarism which is perhaps the most hideous state of affairs we can conceive.

Here, however, we ought to anticipate certain objections, whose weight and scope it would be rash to underestimate. Is not the notion of the person, whether as defined by the Kantian tradition or by the more or less hybrid conceptions which to some extent derive from that tradition, fundamentally rather like the devitalized residue—one might even say the morbidly hardened residue—of a belief that has become exhausted? Ought we not to admit that if the notion of the human person is still capable of inspiring respect it is only to the degree in which that notion profits from the aura which surrounds the notion of a creature formed in the image of his Creator? No doubt Kant and the Kantians are very far from justifying in this way the respect which they claim for the human person, and in the case at least of the author of *The Critique of Practical Reason* himself, it is starting, rather, from the person considered as autonomous subject that such a philosophy claims to arrive at a religion to which the conscience can decently subscribe. But it is impossible to attach oneself exclusively to the letter of a philosophy, and still less can one attach onself to the elaborated expression which it claims to give of itself. A mode of thinking like that of Kant, or even of his most faithful disciples, cannot be separated from a kind of atmosphere in which it was able to develop; that atmosphere is more or less what Jean Guitton, in our time, has studied under the name of 'mentality' or what English thinkers call 'the mental climate', or 'the climate of ideas'. It would probably be no exaggeration to say that it is from such an atmosphere that any mode of thinking draws the air which it must have if it is to go on living. Nobody can deny that the vital atmosphere of Kantianism was one of Christianity and even of Christian pietism. But it is impossible not to see that under a multiplicity of influences, of which some at least have certainly been usefully charted by Marxian analysis, that atmosphere has been to-day transformed. That being so, is it not reasonable to ask whether the ideas of Kantianism are not themselves doomed to perish since that fluid ambiance, if I might describe it so, which was necessary to them has disappeared? In this connection, we cannot allow too much importance to the impact of Nietzsche: if 'God is dead', if the notion of the creature conceived in the image of God therefore lapses at the same time, must we not draw the full conclusion from these premisses, and acknowledge that the idea of the human person is to-day without roots, that it is a survival, and can at the very most be treated only in an academic and anaemic way? Perhaps there is no more serious problem than this. But we ought to guard against a possible source of confusion. In dealing with this problem the philosopher is really in his own territory, really at home. As I have said already, prophecy is not his business. But more than at any other time his task to-day must be a task of discernment.

We have first to consider a question of fact, which must be examined and even explored with the accuracy and courage of a surgeon who is attempting to determine the nature and limits of a lesion.

It seems to me obvious that the techniques of degradation could only have come into being on the basis of a situation which implied the radical, though not yet always the explicit, denial of that character of sacredness which Christianity has always attributed to the human being. If many of us to-day are irresistibly tempted to declare, 'Man is in his death-throes', that way of grasping things is to all appearances vitally connected with Nietzsche's assertion: 'God is dead'. This idea could be developed at length, notably through a research into that mental climate of materialism which has undergone such a strange modification, as I have often remarked, since the end of the nineteenth century. Most of the materialists of that century were still men who went on behaving as if they held the religious beliefs which they declared that they had lost. The fact was that they benefited, without being aware of it, from a Christian atmosphere around them. To-day, one may say that this is no longer the case and that, on the contrary, the materialist tends to live more and more like a materialist; and we are beginning to know what that means.

But a problem of decisive importance arises here; that of knowing what attitude, in so far as we remain conscious beings, in so far as we remain and wish to remain free beings, we ought to take up towards this chain of events. It is essential, indeed, to notice that no chain of events can impose upon us a judgment of value either about itself or about its significance. But let me be more precise: there is no doubt a temptation—and this was what I had in mind just now when I spoke of sliding round the problem or letting oneself be carried off one's course by the current—to let oneself be taken in tow by the event and to confer on it a hall-mark, a stamp of validity. But it is enough for us to think of this temptation *as* a temptation for us to be able to disengage ourselves from the vice in which otherwise we risk being clamped. I mean that our historical situation itself becomes transformed as soon as we are on our guard against what one might call the fascination of the event as such, or at least of the sufficiently large-scale event. A really great event has more often than not a dangerous tendency to make us evaluate all preceding events in the light of our appreciation of what is happening now. This could be specially vividly seen in 1940. At that time, in France, there were a great many people of feeble spirit who saw in our disaster something like a last judgment in miniature, and at the present time we can be certain that if—which God forbid!—a sudden rising of the Soviet waters should come pouring over the West, we should witness the same phenomenon on a much vaster scale, since in this case the ideology which would favour such an interpretation has already been worked out in detail. It is therefore at this very moment, taking advantage of the fact that, though a kind of panic is already making itself manifest, a cool and firm attitude still remains possible, that we ought to call upon our powers of reflection to exorcize, if I dare put it so, this nascent fatalism. We ought to find it very useful, in this connection, to think over what happened in the case of German National Socialism: to remember how strong the temptation was, not on one particular occasion but at several repeated crises, to believe that Nazism had won the day. Let us think of what our state of mind may have been on the eve of El Alamein and while there was still no certain ground for affirming that Stalingrad would hold out to the end.

It is not the case, however, that the two situations are identical. Whatever judgment one may make about Communism, there can be no doubt that its meaning and its scope are incomparably greater than those of Hitlerism: and we can see very clearly how it is that minds lacking adequate intellectual and moral fortification can sincerely imagine that Communism is moving in the direction of historical progress, where Nazism corresponded to a regressive mode of thought. Yet it may be, for all that, that the contrast between Communism and Hitlerism is much more superficial than people would like to believe. I am profoundly convinced that the very expression 'in the direction of historical progress' corresponds to an extremely vague or at least equivocal notion and one that a mode of thinking which remains its own master owes it to itself to break down into its component parts.

For some years past, writers have been recalling attention to a number of prognostications formulated generally by the great French Liberal thinkers of the last century, above all by de Tocqueville, but also by that remarkable and too much neglected social critic, Emil Montaigu. I will quote here a few lines from the latter writer which are to be found in

Gonzague de Reynold's book, *Le Monde Russe*; this completely prophetic passage, for which unfortunately de Reynold does not give an exact reference, was written at some period after the French Commune. 'One day', Montaigu asks, 'and in conditions that will be fearful for Europe, are we not likely to see Russia taking up once more her schemes of universal domination and invasion: schemes whose realization democracy, according to its own admission, is fostering? Who is the hidden Attila, who is the unknown Tamburlaine, who has been dreaming of such a notion? These names are perfectly in place here, for these schemes have to do with nothing less than the conquest of the civilized world. This is war, war openly declared, not war involving merely this or that isolated cause, nor merely this or that country, but war involving all causes and all countries at once. And notice here the great step forward that the Revolution has just taken on that path of universality to which it is committed. In this field, not only are the claims universal; the strategy and the tactics are universal, too. Formerly, in the wars which democracy let loose, only one region would be interested in the outcome of the battle. Now, on the contrary, the repose of all Europe is involved in the chances of each of democracy's conflicts. This doctrine tells us flatly that democracy is a single entity, ruled by a single desire, a single will, a single interest; that England, Germany, France, Belgium, are merely the names of places where democracy intends to fight its future battles, the geographical expressions that will serve to recall the good or bad luck that befalls democracy in the course of that struggle. Not less than half of civilized mankind is proposing to fling itself on the other half and is, moreover, frankly admitting that purpose. If there is not a kind of greatness in all this, there is at least something as gigantic as one could wish for. Does not all this, in any case, transcend the dreams of the loftiest ambition or the most unbridled fancy? Here we have democracy taking over the role of those great conquerors against whom its teachers used so violently to set themselves, and openly aspiring to universal empire. Democracy not only rejects everything that is not itself: it announces that it will accept nothing but itself and will not even leave us the liberties of Jews or Christians in a Moslem country. The new garments democracy is wearing are, in fact, those of an Islam converted to materialism: democracy no longer proposes to liberate mankind from all tyranny, it instead brings its own tyranny; it no longer proposes to us that all beliefs should be tolerated, it brings its own intolerant law, it demands our obedience to its domination, it has started out on the road which all great forces, drunk with their own power, have moved along—a road at the end of which they always find only defeat and the grave.'

Such a thrilling prediction as this is not an isolated statement. A few years earlier Donoso Cortès, whose work Louis Veuillot was to introduce into France, was announcing the coming of 'a great anti-Christian empire, that would be a colossal empire of the demagogue, an empire governed by a plebeian of satanic grandeur, the man of sin'. Though with less precision, Tocqueville in his *Recollections* foresees the danger, and what shall we say of these words of Carnot spoken on the 17th of June, 1868, from the tribune of the Legislative Assembly: 'If Russia were some day to realize her dream of invading the whole Slav world, she would lie against Europe with such a weight that Europe would be reduced to a subordinate position. And also—do not let us deceive ourselves on this point—in such a case it would not be the Slav element that would predominate, it would be the Muscovite element: and the civilization of Asia, with Moscow to lead it, would be triumphing over the civilization of Europe'. Without any exaggeration at all, one may say that, by ways that could not at that time be imagined and thanks to an ideology whose principles had not then been fully worked out, or made perfectly clear, the event has resoundingly justified the predictions of these men of clear judgment. But what has become perfectly clear to-day is that it is only through fratricidal wars between Western and imperfectly Westernized powers that the realization of such terrible prophecies has been made possible.

But there is one point which is certain and which is, indeed, the only point strictly relevant to my argument. The men whom I have quoted, and who all possessed that cool and firm judgment whose general collapse to-day we so much deplore, carefully refrained from giving their predictions the value of a moral command. They did not say that what they foresaw *ought* to happen. Their predictions were, if I may put it so, nothing more than a logical extension to the future, an extrapolation, of their observations on the current situation. When they uttered such terrible predictions, they left their own natural attitudes, their tastes and preferences, out of the argument. Let us agree, of course, that it was easier for them to do so than for ourselves, since they were still at a distance from the event whose coming they foresaw. It may be that good political eyesight has almost inevitably to be, apart from a few really negligible exceptions, of the long-sighted type; in politics perhaps we can only see clearly at a distance. Proximity blurs everything, if only because it encourages that fear and greed which are at the bottom, after all, of all our errors of political judgment: it is certainly fear and greed that are at the bottom of a kind of movement for a 'change of front' which I can see stirring in many sections of Western opinion to-day, and I should add that the presence of such motives is in itself enough to render the movement suspect. One is just as suspicious of it as of that 'examination of conscience' to which so many men betook themselves so precipitately in 1940: perhaps less preoccupied, fundamentally, with 'getting straight with themselves' than with obtaining the indulgence of the conqueror.

Yet we ought to make a distinction here, and it appears to me to be a very important one, between men who have reached maturity and young people who, having known the old order only in its phase of decomposition, may imagine—in a rather naive fashion, certainly—that that old order was in itself lacking in all positive values. Their ignorance, on the one hand, and the perfectly justified feeling of indignation that certain all too glaring injustices inspire in them, on the other, may combine to make them believe that there is not even a choice of one of several courses open to them and that, failing suicide, their one possible course is to adapt themselves for good or ill to a new order, whose defects the more clear-sighted and the more honest of them cannot fail to be aware of, but which, at the cost of a good deal of wastage through wear and tear, ought after all in the end to be able to satisfy certain aspirations that cannot be stifled for ever. And here again we come up against this formidable notion of 'the meaning of history', of 'the direction of historical progress', of a slope which we have to climb; it will even be added, if we bring out the final implications of the notion, that, since other means of persuasion have proved inadequate, it is impossible not to use force to subdue those who claim the right to go against the historical current or resist the historical drive.

Such a claim that the coercive use of force in matters of opinion can be justified seems not only dangerous in itself, but in complete contradiction to the implications of the idea of the human person, as that was accepted almost without discussion at the end of the last century and even during the first quarter of this. What is now more or less explicitly stated, as a principle, is that the human person has no right to respect except in so far as he consents to submit his acts to what one might call the ruling of history. But one has only to state such premisses in order to realize their monstrous nature. In reality, this regulative power does not belong to history, which is not really an entity, but to men who may be nothing more than tyrants and, let me add, criminals, and who present themselves as the executive agents of this strange, ridiculous divinity. But this investiture—that is the only word that is suitable—just *who* has conferred it upon them? One is really making a fool of oneself if one pretends they have been invested with this authority by history itself. Such a phrase is not a thought, but only the simulacrum of a thought, since history is only an abstraction. Nor can we speak seriously of their being invested with this power by general agreement, by a consensus of opinion, since we know that the groups we are thinking of are active minorities; to grasp that fact, it is enough to remember what a minority the Nazis were when they started, or what the Bolsheviks were at the beginning of the Russian revolution. The truth is, a small number of fanatics, forming a compact group, lacking in all scruples, when it has to do with an amorphous human mass, depressed by hunger, weakened by inner divisions, and so on, has in our world to-day a very good chance, if it makes a proper use of propaganda and terror, of exercising that magnetic power whose frightful consequences we have been able to witness in the last thirty years. At the same time, one must add that the intellectuals—particularly the failures and the embittered—will always find a way of giving such movements the sort of fallacious justification that, in spite of everything, they still need if they are to impose on weak minds. Here we have a whole set of operations vitally connected with each other, whose true nature it is the duty of reflective thinking to explore. That, and that alone, is the true face of what is ambitiously called 'the meaning of history' or 'the direction of historical progress'.

But from this point of view we can see very clearly how scandalous the claim is that, to a scarecrow of this sort, we ought to sacrifice the fundamental liberties of the human person. We have above all, of course, to protect ourselves from the power of intimidation that emanates from certain words to which, by a very strange transference, there has been attached to-day something of that sacred value which belongs to the rites and ceremonies of religion. But it is, of course, precisely against such a transference itself that we should be on our guard. No task imposes itself to-day with more urgency than that of a reduction to the lay, the secular level of the principles upon which the false religions of our time are based. I say 'false religions' and these words mean just this: the usurpation by an ideology, which has always, in spite of appearances to the contrary, its sources in human passion, of a transcendency which can belong only to the Uncreated. We ought to add, and this is of the greatest importance, that only a recognition of real transcendency can allow human liberty to persist. And conversely one might say that the note of false transcendency is the attack which it represents upon that same liberty.

It will be objected, no doubt, that revealed religions have themselves often been strikingly marked by abuses of the sort which I have just been denouncing. Not only do I not thrust this objection aside, I make it my own without a shadow of hesitation, and I will say without making any bones about it that a kind of clerical oppression, of which there are plenty of examples around us to-day, amounts to real treason against the essential nature of Christianity: Christianity can only denounce the false religions of which I have spoken on condition of acknowledging and condemning the perversion to which it remains itself exposed in so far as it is constrained to take on institutional forms. The Church, of course, is a divine as well as a human institution but it is under its human, all too human, aspect that, especially in so far as it risks succumbing to the temptations born from pride, it may give rise to such aberrations.

What makes the task of the Christian thinker difficult and even agonizing at the present time is that he has to set his face against two opposite tendencies at once. On the one hand, he must set it against this idolatry of history, in the Hegelian manner, which must be regarded as fundamentally a fraud. On the other, he must set it against reactionary doctrines (in the sense in which the idea of being a 'reactionary' is least defensible), doctrines often springing from ignorance and fear, which lead to a misunderstanding of what is perhaps most valuable in the achievements of contemporary philosophy. These achievements are linked to an undeniably deeper penetration into the very notion of freedom and everything more or less directly connected with freedom. But it must be said that freedom and everything connected with it are as much called into question, as strongly threatened, from one side as from the other. As always happens, moreover, it can be observed that between two diametrically opposed errors, even if they are fighting against each other or believe they are fighting against each other, an alliance for practical purposes is being brought into being. In fact, nothing can serve Communism's purpose better than the spirit of social and religious reaction, and I should add that nothing can be more effectively exploited by atheists than a clericalism which has the tendency to make of God an autocrat served by a priestly caste whose interests are linked with those of dictatorship.

I am, of course, not unaware of the disquieting and superficially even discouraging character of such a diagnosis. But it has, I think, the great advantage of helping us, by the very strength of the reaction it evokes in us, to choose the only path that is open to us if we want to avoid complicity, not merely in a catastrophe, but in the greatest crime which mankind has ever committed against itself.

Let me make myself clear. There can be no question here of my attempting to define anything at all resembling a political line of action. What we have to do with is rather an inner attitude; but this inner attitude cannot remain at the stage of a mere attitude, it must find expression in deeds, and that according to the situation in which each of us finds himself: I mean by that, that this is not a matter, as is unfortunately so often the habit of intellectuals, of our thrusting ourselves into fields in which we are wholly without authority, by signing appeals, manifestos, and so on. I am not giving a distorted emphasis to my own point of view when I say that this sort of thing is too often at the moral level of the petty confidence trick. But on the other hand it is within the scope of each of us, within his own proper field, in his profession, to pursue an unrelaxing struggle for man, for the dignity of man, against everything that to-day threatens to annihilate man and his dignity. It is perhaps above all in the field of the law, in the field of the legal rights of the person, that this struggle ought to be carried on, for we must recognize that the very notion of law, in this sense, is no longer acknowledged, no longer understood. The men of my own generation can bear witness that in this realm a collapse has taken place of which, thirty or forty years ago, nobody would have been able even to conceive. And here again we find the same phantasm, the same 'crowned ghost' which I have been so incessantly denouncing: I mean the idea of a 'meaning of history', a 'direction of historical progress' as constituting the criterion in the name of which certain human beings are to be preserved or even set on high for admiration and others thrust aside, which is to say, eliminated.

Examples could be multiplied. I shall confine myself to recalling the case of the special courts to deal with collaborationists that were set up in France in the years following the Liberation. In these courts, the most elementary rules of law were literally trampled underfoot. They had the impudence to set up juries on which there were sitting people whose competence to give a verdict on this subject ought to have been denied—I mean the victims of collaborationist activity, or their relatives; moreover, it was for the very reason for which their competence as jurymen ought to have been denied that they were granted the right to judge men who they felt had injured them and who had, for that matter, very often been arrested only as a result of anonymous denunciations. If one had space enough, and were not in danger of being too rapidly stifled by disgust and horror, one would have to recall the way in which a certain section of the press, in full agreement, alas, with certain elements in our Government of that time, sought to justify these shameful practices. In abstract language, one might say that what was being sanctioned by official and public approval in this case was the monstrous principle of *inequality* before the law, or, in fact, the very negation of law itself. For we ought to maintain it as an axiom that law and equality before the law are corollaries, and that one cannot attack one without destroying the other. But as soon as the cult of history, of historic dynamism, and so on, comes into the argument, these notions collapse and with them everything, perhaps, that has been denoted by the term civilization.

I say 'civilization': and I should certainly hesitate to speak of 'Christian civilization'. The latter is an expression which has been dangerously misused and to which, in our present circumstances, it is probably dangerous to have recourse without very many qualifications whose general effect will be to rob the words of their primary meaning. What I will say, without pausing to give it great emphasis, is that even if in the present conflict we have to place ourselves on the side of the United States—and it seems to me that there can be no doubt that we have to do so—still, that does not authorize us to say in a simple and straightforward way that the United States is the champion of Christian civilization; for after all, from many points of view, the 'way of life' practised and preached across the Atlantic is very far from appearing in conformity to the demands of the Gospels. All that one can say, all that one can concede, is that on the American side, freedom, in spite of everything, does retain opportunities which in the other camp, for an indefinite period, appear to be completely lost. That is enough to dictate our choice to us, if we have to choose—which in a certain sense is not the case; but at the same time let us admit that the question has to be stated in terms which exclude anything at all resembling 'the crusading spirit'. One should notice also that in such a world as ours, such a world as ours has become, that phrase, 'the crusading spirit', cannot fail to awaken mistrust. It seems inseparable from a warlike spirit to which it is our duty, whether it is awakened in our own hearts or those of others, to oppose, in so far as it is possible to us, a rigorous rejection—which is not, however, to say that the word 'neutrality', of which some sections of opinion in France have made such a rash use during the past few years, retains any currently relevant meaning. In fact it is between a criminal cult of war and a cult of neutrality which, besides being chimerical, to-day smells of treason, that we have to hack for ourselves the narrowest of paths.

Very simply, I will say that if we felt ourselves alone in the world, without God, the task would appear impracticable: for my own part, I fully believe that I should be tempted to abandon it and that at certain moments the temptation to kill myself might perhaps become irresistible. However, we must come back here to what I was saying earlier. Taken literally, Nietzsche's formula, 'God is dead', is not only blasphemous, it is false. And the same must be said of contemporary caricatures of that formula, particularly, of course, of the blasphemies of Sartre and his school. The freedom which we have to defend in its extremity, is not the freedom of Prometheus defying Jupiter; it is not the freedom of a being who could exist or would claim to exist *by himself*. For years past I have not wearied of repeating that freedom is nothing, it makes itself as nothing at what it believes to be the moment of its triumph, unless, in a spirit of complete humility, it recognizes that it has a vital connection with grace: and when I speak of grace, I am not using the word in any abstract or secularized sense, I am thinking of the grace of the living God, that God, alas, whom every day gives us so many chances to deny and whom fanaticism insults—even where fanaticism, far from denying God, claims to find its authority in God's name.

CHAPTER III

THE REINTEGRATION OF HONOUR

COMING home the other evening from an excellent Bach concert, I thought to myself, 'Here is something that restores to one a feeling that one might have thought lost, or perhaps something more than a feeling, an assurance: the assurance that it is an honour to be a man'. It is important to notice that everything seems to be in alliance to-day to destroy this notion of human honour, as to destroy all other notions that reflect an aristocratic morality. People affect to believe that an aristocracy can only be a caste and that the caste-system as such is a mode of existence condemned by history. Now, while we may readily agree that a closed caste-system appears to us to-day as something indefensible, on the other hand we must utterly deny that the idea of aristocracy implies any system of this sort. We should also, of course, note that the way is being visibly prepared for the coming of a kind of world oligarchy, that of 'the managers' in Burnham's sense, the technocrats. Yet it is very doubtful whether such an oligarchy can be regarded as an aristocracy, since one does not see on what genuinely spiritual principle it would claim to base itself.

What sort of a thing is this 'honour' of which the awareness was awakened in me the other night after hearing a few concertos by Bach? It is certainly not easy to make its nature clear; but it seems to me that we have to bring in the idea of an immediate awareness of a kind of fundamental straightness; and as always in such cases, to clarify our notion, we are forced in the first instance to think of it in terms of what is contrary to it.

What the notion of honour seems radically to exclude, then, is anything at the level of accommodation or connivance; at the level of flattery; and also at the level of ambiguity or equivocation, in so far as a perverted mind may be led deliberately to cultivate these. I mean that the idea of honour is linked to that of a man's word and also to the fact that his word should have a single, plain meaning. But it is just this, perhaps, that is the note of an aristocracy in the only acceptable sense of the word—the kind of aristocracy which may not only lack material resources but be unable to boast of noble ancestry. If the Spanish people, for instance, are so generally respected and admired by those who have come in contact with them, is that not precisely because, in spite of their well-known poverty, they have retained that native quality and the pride that goes with it? The pride I am thinking of is something very different from the pride, the arrogance, which is a deadly sin; though it is often in danger of being confused with it. It seems to me that a 'proper pride' of this sort is always connected with the sense of an, as it were, innate and inalienable independence; and such a pride therefore stands in strange contrast with that spirit of claiming one's due which is so typical of democracies. For that spirit is out to claim not *what it has*, but *what it ought to have*. Now, for the man of 'proper pride' this contrast between what he has and what he ought to have does not exist; he would feel, in a sense, that he was lowering himself by claiming his due.

It is not to be denied that such pride may be the source of a stiffness, a lack of suppleness, not very compatible with the conditions of social life, as we tend to conceive them to-day. We ought also to acknowledge without any reserves that if, from the point of view of social justice, real progress in certain very restricted fields has been achieved, that has been possible only because during the last hundred years the workers have repeatedly claimed their due from the so-called directing classes, classes at most times only too ready to refuse to allow their privileges even to be discussed. But it cannot be denied, on the other hand, that the development of the spirit of claiming one's due can coincide with a kind of moral degradation. To be certain of this, I have only to think of these friendly gatherings of university teachers at which the serious technical problems arising out of the job of teaching itself are never touched on, but only questions of salary increases and cost-of-living allowances. In a quite general sense, it does seem to me undeniably true that by a sad paradox the sense of professional honour has tended to diminish to the extent to which the members of each profession have become aware of their power as a pressure-group; and one expression of this fact is the extent to which what one can only call collective blackmail has become a generalized phenomenon during the last ten or twenty years.

From another but not unconnected point of view, we can see that the man of 'proper pride' is a man who does not allow his word to be doubted. For *his word is himself*, one might be tempted to say that it is his only real possession, and honour is just the awareness of this indefectible quality, of one's word as being what is called in equations an invariable. From this fact one might infer that honour is always linked to a deep sense, a sense that cannot be uprooted, of *being;* for between being and the word there does exist, as Heidegger has shown in Germany and that profound but little-known thinker, Brice Parain, in France, an irrefragable unity. One should not draw the conclusion from this, of course, that honour in itself implies anything resembling an articulate religious faith. Among the best of the Spanish anarchists, on the contrary, honour was able to ally itself with an atheism which in its depths, for that matter, was perhaps nothing more than a mere refusal; the rejecting of a condition of feudal servitude which, of course, a sufficiently evolved theology would have recognized as incompatible with the fundamental principles of the Christian faith, with the freedom of the children of God. There is no more serious problem than that of knowing how Church membership, while retaining its strictly religious value, can avoid degenerating into a condition of feudal servitude incompatible with honour.

It must, to be sure, seem strange to illustrate a reflection set going by hearing the music of Bach with examples partly drawn from the life of the Spanish soul. But in thinking out a situation so complex and in some ways so agonizing as that of contemporary man, there may be an advantage in starting off from several different focal topics at once. Between these it will not require very profound reflection to discover a secret kinship.

Into Bach, it seems to me, as into the very structure of the Spanish soul, we must see how impossible it is to introduce anything like the opposition, so current among French rationalists, between reason and faith. In one sense, no music can be more satisfying to the reason than that of Bach, but on the other hand this satisfaction, which so soon transcends itself to become a higher state, obviously represents a response to some gift which reason reduced to its mere self would never have been able to lavish on us. In fact, for that matter, *can* reason ever really *give* us anything? It can only exploit and transform—and sometimes also reduce and dissolve, the latter in the case where its exercise becomes purely critical. But it is false to claim that, because of its own status, reason is in some sense obliged to defend itself against gifts whose source it does not know and to refuse them rather as one might refuse contraband merchandise. Reason, though it recognizes itself as overwhelmed by the music of Bach, expands itself, on the contrary, to welcome that light; for, in its depths, reason has a presentiment, though a very indistinct one, that this light is of the same nature as reason itself, and I am ready to affirm that reason makes it a point of honour to proclaim this identity, *to whose origin and nature nevertheless it has no clue.*

Honour in such a case is really linked to gratitude—a wonderful word, and a word into whose deeper sense, it seems to me, thinkers have too rarely penetrated. In what sense does the ungrateful man sin against honour? Is it not that he is in some sense a betrayer, that he breaks a certain tie, profiting basely from the fact that his benefactor—let us ignore for the moment certain rather unpleasant overtones which that word may have—has carefully avoided asking him for any sort of acknowledgement of his debt? But the man of honour will feel himself all the more under an obligation just because that official acknowledgment of a debt does not exist; he would consider it an act of utter baseness to say that he feels his obligation is nothing because nothing has been asked of him. It seems to him that the exact converse is true. One might say, I think, that an ethic of honour is not only an ethic of fidelity but that it is also an ethic of gratitude, and that, in the extreme case, this gratitude assumes an ontological character, since it is a gratitude for having been allowed to exist, that is to say, fundamentally, for having been created. It is against such an ethic or such a metaphysics that the nihilist is sinning when he declares that he never asked to be alive: there, we are at the roots of the impiety which tends to diffuse itself generally to-day even into the bonds of family life themselves—and at the roots also, on the other hand, of a very dangerous attitude in parents, which is, as it were, an attempt to counterbalance this impiety, and which manifests itself sometimes as a weak and flattering softness towards their children, deriving from a bad conscience, or from an actual sense of shame which seems to attach itself to-day to the fact that one has given life, that one has literally inflicted life on somebody who did not ask for it.

One might pursue similar reflections about the disappearance of the sense of hospitality to-day, at least in the countries which have been submerged by technical progress. We ought, of course, to be accurate in our way of stating this: to be sure, famous visitors, well-known scholars, writers, or artists are usually very well received in all countries. But by the sense of hospitality, I mean above all the sort of piety which is shown in the East to the unknown guest—simply because he is a guest, because he has entrusted himself to a man and his dwelling.

But these are the very bonds between man and man that are tending to disappear in a world where individuals, reduced to their abstract elements, are more and more merely juxtaposed, and where the only hierarchies that remain are founded either on money or on educational qualifications whose human significance is practically nil.

Honour, in every case, appears to be linked to a certain noble and generous simplicity in the fundamental human relationships.

CONCLUSION

THE UNIVERSAL AGAINST THE MASSES (II)

WHAT sort of general conclusion can the arguments of a book like this imply? There can be no question, certainly, of anything resembling a prophecy. From man's point of view—and that expression is pleonastic, since there is no point of view that is not man's, that does not start with man—it must be said as firmly as possible that everything is not finished, that we have not 'had our chance', that fatalism is a sin and a source of sin. The philosopher is not a prophet, he is no prophet in any sense, and that means above all that it is not for him to put himself in the place of God. To do so, at his own level of thought, would not only be an absurdity but an act of sacrilege. Yet it is important to remember, here, that the prophet himself, the true prophet, never puts himself in the place of God, but effaces himself so that God may speak, which is something very different. However, that sublime vocation is not that of the philosopher. To-day, the first and perhaps the only duty of the philosopher is to defend man against himself: to defend man against that extraordinary temptation towards inhumanity to which—almost always without being aware of it—so many human beings to-day have yielded.

But a tragic difficulty arises here: for a century past, and perhaps for longer, man has been led to call his own nature into question, and this has been necessarily so from the moment in which he no longer acknowledged himself to be a creature made in the image of God. That, no doubt, is the fundamental reason why what Nietzsche called the 'Death of God' could only be followed, and almost immediately followed, by the death-throes of man. Let us make our meaning clear: something which, for the thinker, is *brought into question* is, for the non-thinker, almost bound to become pure negation. Self-questioning and suspended judgment seem almost incompatible with the demands of action: think of Shakespeare's Prince Hamlet. Thus the man who is non-religious—which is to say, the man who has broken his bonds—becomes the man who rejects, who refuses. But we have to go further into this dialectical process, which, for that matter, is suffered rather than thought. The man who rejects, if he is perfectly consistent with himself, will be the integral nihilist. But for reasons which have to do with the very conditions and, as it were, the structure of existence, the integral nihilist can only be an extreme case, an exception which fundamentally is not a practicable one. Let us beware, in any case, of attempted discourse about an ideal single being, the man who rejects: such singleness only exists subjectively. It is what speaks, not what can be objectively spoken of. What can be objectively spoken of is *men*, the objective is plural. It is only *between* men who reject that there can come into being what I should like to call unnatural bonds—I am contrasting them with the natural bonds that link together members of the same family or citizens of the same city, when family or city is in a healthy state.

It is starting from such observations that we ought to re-read Dostoevsky's *The Possessed*, one of the most profound novels—and one of the most essentially prophetic novels—that have ever been written. What I really mean is this: in the world that we know—I make this qualification, for there would be no point in referring to other types of civilization, to which we have not the key—human beings can be linked to each other by a real bond only because, in another dimension, they are linked to something which transcends them and comprehends them in itself. Now, the men who reject have broken with that superior principle, and it is in vain that they attempt to replace it by a fiction wholly lacking in ontological attributes and in any case projected into the future. In spite of all the phrases we make use of in our attempt to confer an appearance of reality on such fictions, all that actually happens is that a reality is displaced and a fiction replaces it.

But what happens at this point is something extremely serious. We know very well that abstractions cannot remain at the stage of mere abstraction. It is just as if they took on concrete life; though an abnormal and unhealthy life, which we could properly compare to that of a cancer-tissue. It is experience alone that can throw light on when, where, and how such life is able to take shape. We should have to look, in the first place, into just how the mass condition is able to come into being, particularly in great urban and industrial agglomerations; and secondly into how these masses—to whom we must refuse all ontological dignity, that is, we must not consider them as having substantial being—can be galvanized and magnetized, invariably, as it would seem, by fanatical groups growing up round a nucleus of dictatorship. I am myself neither a sociologist nor an historian, and so must be broad and sketchy here. However, it would be necessary to transcend such data as history and sociology might provide us with in order to isolate, if not exactly the laws, at least the more or less constant conditions, of a social dynamism which imitates life but reaches its climax only in what we ought rather to call death: that is, in servitude and terror. And no doubt it is from that night of servitude and terror that we ought then to seek once more to rise, like a diver coming up to the surface, if we wished to rediscover the human in its dignity and plenitude.

But there is another aspect of this topic on which it is important now to insist. Techniques, as I have repeatedly said, cannot be considered as evil in themselves, quite the opposite. Nevertheless, we ought to recognize that unless we make a truly ascetic effort to master techniques and put them in their proper subordinate place, they tend to assemble themselves, to organize themselves, around the man who rejects. It is a mysterious and significant fact about our contemporary world that nihilism is tending to take on a technocratic character, while technocracy is inevitably nihilist. I say, *technocracy* is: there is an absolute distinction in theory between *technocracy* and *the proper sphere of techniques*, even though in practice the distinction may appear to-day to have reached vanishing point. However, it is no less obvious that this connection, between nihilism and technocracy, is not a patent one, and no doubt it is of its essence not to be so. Nothingness or mere negation is, as it were, the secret which technocracy jealously hides in its heart, and this under whatever aspect technocracy presents itself to us. In the end—but only in the end—it is permissible to pass the same verdict of condemnation on American technocracy as on that at which the Soviet world is aiming. But I should add that such a condemnation based, in this case, on a possible extreme development of existing American tendencies must arouse suspicion, just because it is too easy. It is a sort of condemnation at which intellectuals excel, just because they are frivolous and usually without concrete and circumstantial knowledge of what they are talking about.

From this certainly rather confused bundle of observations it is, I think, possible to pick out a number of more precise warnings that each of us could take to heart.

The most urgent and imperative of all these warnings might be put in the following way. As soon as I start thinking, —and by thinking I mean reflecting, here—I am forced not only to take notice of the extreme danger in which the world to-day stands but also to become aware of the responsibilities which fall upon myself in such a situation. This should be strongly emphasized: for the very act of thinking, as the whole history of philosophy shows us, brings with it a temptation, that of detachment, that of *self-insulation*. But this temptation only persists where reflection has not yet deployed itself in every possible dimension. I discover that it is a temptation, and by the same act I surmount it, as soon as I have understood that what I call the self is not a source but an obstacle; it is not from the self, it is *never* from the self that the light pours forth, even though, through an illusion which is hard to dissipate, it is of the very nature of our ego to take itself as a projector when it is only a screen. The ego is essentially pretentious, it is its nature to be a pretender in every sense of the word.

But when we have recognized this fundamental responsibility, what sort of effort should we make to face it? In other words, what is the first ethical commandment to which I ought, as a philosopher, to conform? Without any possible doubt it is that I ought not to sin against the light. But what exact meaning are we to give to this term 'light'? I do not say to this metaphor of light; for in fact we are not in possession of any word in relation to which the term can be judged metaphorical. The expression at the beginning of the Gospel according to St John, 'That was the true Light, which lighteth every man that cometh into the world', defines in the most rigorous fashion and in terms of unsurpassable adequacy what is in fact the most universal characteristic of human existence; one can see that clearly if one adds by way of corollary that man is not man except in so far as that light lights him. And if nevertheless, yielding to an almost uncontrollable inner necessity, we do after all attempt to elucidate the meaning of the word 'light', we shall have to say that it denotes what we can only define as the identity at their upper limit of Love and Truth: we should have to add that a truth which lies below that limit is a pseudo-truth and conversely that a love without truth is in some respects a mere delirium.

We must now ask ourselves what are the still singular and in many ways mysterious conditions under which we can have access to this light? Leaving on one side Revelation properly so called, which has always remained in relation to any thoughts put forward in this work at, as it were, the horizon, I would say that we all have to radiate this light for the benefit of each other, while remembering that our role consists above all and perhaps exclusively in not presenting any obstacle to its passage *through us*. This, in spite of all appearances to the contrary, is an active role: it is an active role just because the self is a pretender, and a pretender whose duty it is to transcend or to destroy its own false claims. This can only be achieved through freedom and in a sense this *is* freedom.

But on our way to these conclusions we have been able to isolate other temptations which we ought to resist. One of the most dangerous and diffused of these is linked to the prestige of numbers (and of statistics). It is at this level of thought that the most sinister collusion takes place between a degraded philosophy and a simple-minded dogmatism deriving from the natural sciences; it seems as if the mind becomes corrupt as soon as it accustoms itself to juggling with numbers that correspond to nothing in the imagination—this is true both of the infinitely great and the infinitely little. To be sure, it would be mere madness to refuse to recognize the necessity, for the astronomer and the physicist in their specialized domains, of such dangerous manipulations. But the danger begins when such methods, which in themselves must always remain open to suspicion, are transferred from such domains to another domain: I mean from a specialized field of thought, which has to make use of special methods, to the field of concrete general activity which is that of man *qua* man. Here we ought to restore in their plenitude the meaning, and the implicit affirmation, of the word 'neighbour'; and at no point does the essential agreement between the Gospels and the results of philosophical reflection more fully reveal its fertility. It is impossible not to allude here to the kind of aberration of which a famous French palaeontologist once gave an example. He is a man who sincerely believes that he is a Christian, but who has succumbed more thoroughly than anyone else to the intoxication of great numbers. On one occasion, when he was dilating on his confidence in world progress, and somebody was trying to call to his attention the case of the millions of wretches who are slowly dying in Soviet labour camps, he exclaimed, so it seems: 'What are a few million men in relation to the immensity of human history?' A blasphemy! Thinking in terms of millions and multiples of millions, he could no longer conceive, except in terms of 'cases', of abstractions, of the unspeakable and intolerable reality of the suffering of the single person—a suffering literally masked from him by the mirage of numbers.

In the foreword to my *Mystery of Being*, I proposed that my thought should henceforth be designated under the name of neo-Socratism. In this context, that description takes on its full meaning. The return to one's neighbour appears to be the real condition of a neo-Socratic approach to being; and I would add that the more we estrange ourselves from our neighbour, the more we are lost in a night in which we can no longer even distinguish being from non-being. But can one fail to see that technocracy consists precisely of making an abstraction of one's neighbour and, in the long run, denying him? I shall remember a remark made to me by a man who has remarkable intellect but one too much contaminated, alas, by the errors of our time! As I was speaking to him of my admiration for so many young French Christians, almost all of middle-class background, who are to-day courageously and under very great difficulties bringing up large families, 'On the contrary', he said vigorously, 'there is nothing to admire. When one is aware of the conclusions recently arrived at by the board set up in the United States to make an estimate of world stocks of primary commodities, this fecundity for which you feel such wondering admiration seems mere madness'. The dramatist in me—and I might add, the comic dramatist—immediately imagined a young couple who, before deciding to start a baby on the way, hurried away to some set of technical experts to discover the state of the harvests in South America or Central Africa. My friend was forgetting that, in France itself, as a result of the accumulated errors of the governmental system, whole fertile regions are being allowed to lie fallow. A family does not have to think on the world scale, it does not have to make its horizon an unlimited one. To think the contrary is to be a technocrat.

I should, of course, be guilty of bad faith if I refused to agree that there is, in fact, a real and terrible problem of possible overpopulation in the world; but is man as he is made to-day capable of facing this problem or even of stating it in acceptable terms? It is, in reality, a problem for a demiurge; but the idea of a human demiurge is self-contradictory, and we are paying a high price for not having recognized that earlier: the price of the low spiritual level at which we find ourselves to-day. For my own part, here I think that the role of the philosopher consists above all in putting men of science and action on their guard against such *hubris:* against, that is, such unmeasured arrogance.

It is our duty not only to make the imprescriptible rights of the universal currently recognized, but also to plot out with the greatest care the terrain on which these rights can be effectively defended. In my introduction to this book, I said that the word 'universal' seems fated to give rise to misunderstandings of the very sort most likely to darken and confuse its real meaning. We are almost irresistibly inclined to understand 'the universal' as that which presents a maximum of generality. But that is an interpretation against which one cannot too strongly react. The best course here is for the mind to seek its support among the highest expressions of human genius—I mean among those works of art which have a character of supreme greatness. Being a musician myself, for instance, I am thinking of the last works of Beethoven. How can anybody fail to see that any sort of notion of generality is quite inapplicable here? On the contrary, if a sonata like Opus 111 or a quartet like Opus 127 introduces us to what is most intimate and I would even say most sacred in our human condition, at the level where that condition transcends itself in a significance which is at once self-evident and beyond any possible formulation, at the same time it addresses itself only to a very restricted number of people, without for that reason at all losing its universal value. We must understand that universality has its place in the dimension of depth and not that of breadth. Shall we say that the universal is accessible only to the individual? There again is a notion about which we must be terribly cautious. We have to reject the atomic just as much as the collective conception of society. Both, as Gustave Thibon has so pregnantly remarked, are complementary aspects of the same process of decomposition—I would say of local mortification.

There can be no authentic depth except where there can be real communion; but there will never be any real communion between individuals centred on themselves, and in consequence morbidly hardened, nor in the heart of the mass, within the mass-state. The very notion of intersubjectivity on which all my own most recent work has been based presupposes a reciprocal openness between individuals without which no kind of spirituality is conceivable.

But this fact has a particular importance from the point of view of action, and it opens up new horizons to us. It is only within groups that are fairly restricted in size and animated by a spirit of love that the universal can really embody itself. From this point of view, it is very important to rehabilitate that aristocratic idea, which has been to-day discredited, for the worst possible reasons, in the name of an egalitaranism that cannot stand up for a moment to critical thought. Only, of course, the content of this idea of aristocracy must be renewed. We ought to think, particularly, of what an aristocracy of craftsmanship might have been; I say 'might have been', for the almost systematic destruction of the craftsman in France to which an idiotic legislation has contributed obliges us, here, to project our conjectures into the past. But it is absolutely necessary that aristocracies should be recreated, for we must face the terrible fact that every levelling process must proceed downwards, to the base of the hierarchy: there is not, and cannot be, such a thing as 'levelling up'. There can be no more serious problem than that of investigating around what centres, what focal points, these new aristocracies can constitute themselves. It is probable that this very worrying problem does not imply an abstract and general solution; there are and only can be the particular cases, groups managing to form themselves according to the circumstances around an institution, a personality, a living idea, and so on.

But there is a complementary remark to be made. In every case such a group runs the risk of shutting itself up in itself and becoming a sect or a 'little clan', and as soon as it does so it betrays the universal value which it is supposed to be embodying. It is therefore the duty of each group to remain in a sort of state of active expectation or availability in relation to other groups moved by a different inspiration, with whom it ought to have fertilizing exchanges of view; and it is on this condition alone that each group can remain a living group and avoid the morbid hardening that results from its becoming the seat of a sort of self-idolatry. This life of the group, moreover, can only develop in time; it has its bearings set towards an achievement outside of time, which it would be futile to seek to anticipate in imagination, but whose joyous presentiment is, as it were, the mainspring of all activity worthy of the name, of all true creation. Such a life is by its very nature one of adventure; it does not exclude risks, it rather presupposes them; and on the other hand the principles of such a life cannot be generalized and put forward as a kind of system. I would say, rather, that what can be reduced to a system is incompatible with the profoundest inner need that animates such a life, and that this need itself implies the mysterious encounter of the mind and heart.

It should be added that it is up to each of us to make what we call a reality of, that is, to incarnate, such guiding ideas as this; for these guiding ideas will be lies if they are not given definite practical shape. It is true to say that there is nobody at all—and I am thinking here at least as much of the most humble lives as of those that attract our attention—who does not find himself placed in a concrete setting in which such incarnation of these guiding ideas is possible and even requisite: there is nobody at all who is not in a position to encourage, within himself and beyond himself, the spirit of truth and love. But one should immediately add the converse proposition: there is nobody at all who is not in a position, through the powers of rejection which he possesses, to put obstacles in the way of such encouragement and thus to maintain in the world a state of blindness, of mutual mistrust, of internal division, that are paving the way for the world's destruction and his own. What is asked of all of us, such as we are—and here truly is what one might call our existential secret—is that we should discover what that sphere is, however restricted it may be, in which our own activity can be vitally connected with that universal purpose, which is the purpose of love and truth in the world. Our error or our fault invariably consists in our wanting to persuade ourselves that no such sphere exists and that our contribution to the task that has to be accomplished in the world cannot amount to anything. An even more serious error consists in denying the existence or the imperativeness of this task and shutting ourselves up in the awareness of a sterile liberty.

I am very far of course from disguising from myself the objections to which this attempt of mine once more to make become conscious of itself, and it exists at the level of thinking in pure abstractions.

During a recent trip to Morocco, I was able to observe with trepidation the incredible misdeeds of which devotees of ideologies can become guilty when, rejecting reality, they claim to judge by their chosen categories even men and events to which these categories are strictly inapplicable. What is tragic—and I touch here for the last time on one of the major themes of this book—is that such abstractions are far from being without practical impact: latent in them are almost infinite possibilities of disorder. Thus I end as I began: the philosopher can help to save man from himself only by a pitiless and unwearying denunciation of the spirit of abstraction. No doubt he will be denounced as a Conservative, a reactionary, possibly even a Fascist—though he knows that it is his duty to denounce Fascism as one of the cancers of democracy—but what does that matter? It is the masses who hurl these accusations at him or, at the most, the man who is only an echo of the masses. But the philosopher knows that the mass itself is a lie and it is *against the mass* and *for the universal* that he must bear witness.